PIERRE FRANEY
COOKS WITH HIS FRIENDS

PIERRE FRANEY
COOKS WITH HIS FRIENDS

WITH RECIPES FROM TOP CHEFS IN FRANCE, SPAIN, ITALY, SWITZERLAND, GERMANY, BELGIUM & THE NETHERLANDS

PIERRE FRANEY

WITH CLAUDIA FRANEY JENSEN

PHOTOGRAPHS BY MARTIN BRIGDALE AND JEAN CAZALS

ARTISAN New York

EDITOR: ANN FFOLLIOTT
PRODUCTION DIRECTOR: HOPE KOTURO

Published in 1997 by Artisan,
a division of Workman Publishing Company, Inc.
708 Broadway
New York, NY 10003-9555

Library of Congress Cataloging-in-Publication Data
Franey, Pierre.
Pierre Franey cooks with his friends :
with recipes from top chefs in France, Spain, Italy, Switzerland, Germany,
Belgium, and the Netherlands / Pierre Franey with Claudia Franey Jensen ;
photographs by Martin Brigdale and Jean Cazals.

Includes index
ISBN 1-885183-60-7
1. Cookery, International. 2. Cooks—Europe. 3. Low-fat diet—
Recipes. I. Jensen, Claudia Franey. II. Title
TX725.A1F67 1997   96-47968
CIP

Printed in Italy
10 9 8 7 6 5 4 3 2 1
First Printing

Au Revoir, Papa

Sad changes come to all of us. For my family and myself, it was saying good-bye to my father, Pierre. He passed away in October 1996, just as he and I were finishing this cookbook together. His absence weighs heavily upon us.

Papa loved the world of food. It was his passion. He found his calling as a young boy growing up in a small village in France. At a very early age, he loved to watch his mother and grandmother cook the family meals. "Pierre, le Gourmand" they would call him. At the age of 14, having decided what he wanted to do with the rest of his life, he left his family in Burgundy to become an apprentice cook in Paris. From that day on, he never stopped cooking. The day he became fatally ill, while crossing the Atlantic on the Queen Elizabeth II, he had just finished a cooking demonstration before a crowd of four hundred people.

When I was a child, Papa was the Executive Chef at Le Pavillon in New York; he worked very long hours six days a week. In spite of that he always cooked the family meal on Sunday, his only day off. For him, it was a pleasure, not a chore. Chopping an onion, sautéing a pork chop, whipping up egg whites, creating a new recipe, was not only a form of relaxation, but an inner need to express himself. His creativity in the kitchen was boundless.

But what made Papa so special was his openness to others. He shared his love of food as well as his incredible knowledge with anyone who asked him. Never one to keep "secrets of the kitchen" to himself, he loved giving advice to anyone who asked. I can't tell you the number of times he was stopped on the road while bicycling for his morning newspaper or while playing petanque with his friends, by strangers seeking his counsel. He was always happy to help out.

I was very honored when he asked me to collaborate on this book with him. Any reservations on my part were swept away by his confidence in my abilities. I will always cherish the time we spent together while traveling around Europe visiting these wonderful chefs and the hours he and I sat side by side while I typed at the computer and he talked about the recipes in the book. His recommendations accompany each recipe and are shared here with you.

At the time of my father's death, a close friend who knew him well wrote to me, "A heart that touches the lives of others lives on forever." I find these words very comforting. And, I believe the same can be said of his talent, which he passed on to his family, friends, and fans through his meals at home, his cookbooks, his cooking shows, and his demonstrations. I like to think that Papa lives on every time someone cooks one of his recipes or refers to one of his cookbooks for some ideas. He will always be with us.

—Claudia Franey Jensen

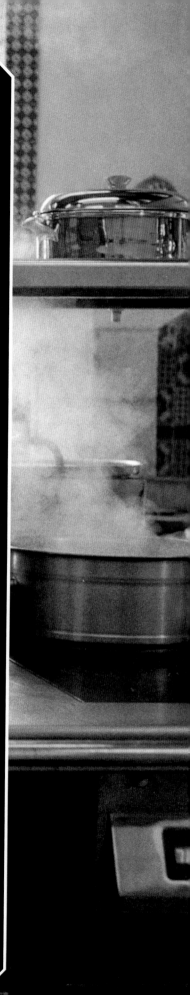

CONTENTS

INTRODUCTION

*I*t was with great delight and a sense of adventure that I embarked on this culinary journey through Europe. Even after sixty years of cooking, I still feel I can learn something new. That's what excites me about the world of food. There are always new chefs with innovative ideas, cooking with new combinations of ingredients; or food producers who have found a more efficient yet healthier way to grow food; or older, established chefs who show a remarkable capability in adapting their cuisines as an increasingly health-conscious clientele come to their restaurants.

Over the years, thanks to my friendship with Craig Claiborne and my affiliation with *The New York Times,* I was introduced to talented chefs and restaurateurs from all over the world. Craig and I frequently worked together in his home in East Hampton, Long Island, playing host to men and women who worked in the top restaurants in their countries. We would spend hours in the kitchen, cooking together, learning from one another, and then sitting down to candlelit dinners, regaling in the results of our mutual efforts. I made many good friends and developed an appreciation of other cuisines. And, in turn, I enjoyed visiting my new friends, eating in their restaurants, and appreciating their ability to cook delicious meals.

Two years ago, after finishing my successful "Cooking in France" series for public television, I felt a real desire to make a television series visiting some of the best chefs in Europe. After all, France is not the only country where one can eat well! I sat down and put together a list of top chefs and restauranteurs in seven European countries—France, Spain, Italy, Switzerland, Germany, the Netherlands, and Belgium. I wanted to see some good friends whose cooking I very much admired. I also wanted to visit several chefs whose cooking I knew only by reputation. I had met some of them in New York City at special dinners at the restaurants of Sirio Maccioni, owner of Le Cirque, and Jean-Jacques Rachou, chef-owner of La Cote Basque.

I got on the phone to explain to these chefs my idea about coming to their restaurants, watching them cook, and our cooking together for television, and they were very interested. But I added a new twist to the program—we had to cook "low fat." These days, people everywhere—young and old—are watching what they eat. Not surprisingly, the chefs became even more enthusiastic. All of them, without exception, have made changes on their menus in recent years because they are conscious of a need to cook with less fat, not only for their clients, but for themselves, too.

It is not only in America that people have become more aware of their what they eat. In my travels around Europe I discovered that chefs there have responded to a need for "lighter cooking." People don't want to eat as much or as heavily as they once did. My friend Michel Guérard was the first to introduce "cuisine minceur" years ago. He began cooking this way simply because he himself wanted to shed a few pounds. Today his three-star restaurant includes a "spa cuisine" menu that combines good nutrition, delicious flavors, and a mixture of dishes that will keep one's daily intake of fat low.

I don't mean to imply that you can't get the traditional dishes, but rather that there is more of a choice now. In Spain, Ferran Adrià of El Bulli on the Costa Brava has developed his own style of cuisine, not necessarily Spanish nor French. He makes great use of the region's specialties and creates dishes inspired by the world around him.

But, we want to enjoy what we eat, too! I now know that one can cook with much less fat and still have a delicious meal. For example, I use egg whites in place of whole eggs when making crab cakes. With far less cholesterol, the egg whites bring a lightness and airiness to the dish and, at the same time, help to bind the ingredients. My long-time friend Paul Bocuse has adapted his cooking as well. He is famous throughout the world for his rich cuisine using cream, butter, and truffles. Paul is gregarious, outspoken, and a real lover of food. Imagine my surprise when I last saw him and he had shed more than 50 pounds. He told me that his desire to lead a healthier life changed the way he cooked for himself and made him develop new ways to prepare the food he loved. He has brought some of these changes to the kitchens of his three restaurants in and around Lyon.

In this book, I bring to you a sampling of recipes from today's top European chefs. They are not only nutritionally sound and low in fat, but also quite simple to make. In addition, I have added some of my own recipes, which I have developed over the last few years with an eye toward lowering the fat content. This is not a "diet" cookbook; some recipes include butter, eggs, milk, and cheese. I cannot cook any other way. But, I have approached these classic recipes using moderate amounts of these high-fat ingredients. You will find that some recipes contain small quantities of butter, which is high in cholesterol and fat, but more of them use small quantities of olive oil, which, although it is pure fat, has no cholesterol and, as recent research indicates, may actually lower blood cholesterol levels. When I can, I substitute egg whites for whole eggs. You will find no cream in my recipes, the meat is rendered of its fat, and I have used a multitude of herbs and spices.

I created some of these recipes during my European tour. I often became inspired when visiting the various local markets and seeing chefs cook in their kitchens and from their gardens. These chefs were unanimous in their belief that good, healthful cooking must be based on fresh local produce. I very much agree and I encourage you to take advantage of the foods that are indigenous to your locality. Fresh herbs are essential to this way of cooking. They are easy to grow and in recent years, they have become much more available in North American greengrocers and supermarkets.

By cooking with less fat, fresh produce, and the right combination of herbs, you will find yourself making tasty meals that quickly satisfy your tastebuds and your stomach. With moderate use of butter, eggs, olive oil, cheese, and milk, you will be able to create a real richness of flavor and you will not have to eat a lot to feel saited. I truly believe that a balanced use of ingredients makes for a more tantalizing meal. It is the intensity of flavor and the right combination of ingredients that will satisfy your appetite. Eat healthy, but eat well!

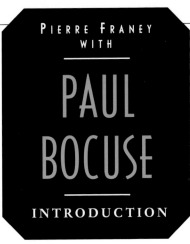
*I*t is perhaps appropriate that I began this journey by boarding a train in Paris and heading straight for Lyon, one of the premier gastronomic centers of France. Located halfway between Paris and the Mediterranean, it sits at the intersection of two major rivers, the Rhône and the Saône. People in Lyon are very serious about their food. Restaurants abound throughout the city, and range from expensive *haute*

cuisine to authentic family-run bistros. Founded in 43 B.C., Lyon was the Roman capital of the province of Gaul. Even today, on a visit through Vieux Lyon (old Lyon), with its narrow, twisting streets and alleyways, one gets a sense of how the city looked in medieval and Renaissance times.

Just five miles north of Lyon, along the banks of the Saône River, is the small, peaceful village of Collonges-au-Mont-d'Or, home of my good friend, the world-renowned chef Paul Bocuse. Paul grew up here, in a family of restaurateurs that goes back sev-

RIGHT: *Pierre watches Paul Bocuse at work in his restaurant's kitchen.*
OPPOSITE: *The world-renowned chef stands in front of the mural that decorates the restaurant exterior.*

eral generations. It all started when one of his ancestors, the wife of a miller, began making meals for the river men who brought sacks of grain to her husband's mill. Paul has fond memories of his youth—working in the kitchen of his family's restaurant, fishing along the Saône with his father, and developing a love of good food. He had classical training in French cuisine, working as an apprentice in the kitchens of well-known restaurants in Lyon, Vienne, and Paris. He then returned to his family's restaurant and soon achieved a three-star rating in the *Guide Michelin*, France's top rating for a restaurant. He has deep respect for the family tradition behind the restaurant—its walls are covered with photographs of the family and of special dinners that have taken place there.

Paul has earned a reputation as the ambassador and biggest promoter of French cuisine. He has traveled extensively around the world and has learned much about other cuisines. Although he is known for his use of rich ingredients such as cream, butter, truffles, and foie gras, Paul has

BELOW: *Paul and Pierre share a meal at the restaurant.* RIGHT: *Restaurant Paul Bocuse, Collonges-au-Mont-d'Or, near Lyon, France.* OVERLEAF: *The exterior of the restaurant presents a trompe l'oeil effect, with its mural* Rue des Grands Chefs, *which pays tribute to great chefs past and present.*

also adapted the way he cooks for his clients as well as himself. He does not believe in "dieting" nor in substituting low-fat versions of ingredients in his recipes. Rather, he takes care to cook with less fat and to eat smaller portions. He says he will never completely give up butter and cream, but when he is watching what he's eating he reduces their quantities by half. He also uses more olive oil. Over a three-year period, he has lost nearly 60 pounds while eating three meals a day. When I visited with him on this trip, he was happy to prepare these dishes that use very little fat.

FROM PAUL BOCUSE

CHICKEN AND VEGETABLES WITH PUFF PASTRY

BLACK SEA BASS WITH A POTATO CRUST AND A LIGHT VINAIGRETTE

FROM PIERRE FRANEY

MACKEREL FILLETS IN WHITE WINE

LEEKS VINAIGRETTE

POTATO-GOAT CHEESE QUICHE

CHEESE PASTRY DOUGH

SPINACH WITH NUTMEG

WATERCRESS AND ENDIVE SALAD WITH WALNUTS

BANANA SHERBET WITH YOGURT AND STRAWBERRY SAUCE

CHICKEN AND VEGETABLES WITH PUFF PASTRY

YIELD: 4 SERVINGS

There is no added fat in this recipe—just what is contained in the puff pastry topping. This is one of Paul Bocuse's favorite dishes served in his restaurant. The chicken and vegetables must be very fresh because it is prepared with no butter or oil to add moisture. If necessary, a small amount of chicken broth or water can be added to the vegetables before sealing the tureen. You should cook this dish in a 3-quart ovenproof soup tureen, about 8 inches in diameter. The tureen, or soupière, should have a solid stem to promote even cooking. If one is not available, use a Dutch oven and place it on a rack in the oven.

1 3½-pound lean free-range chicken

6 thin slices black truffle

Salt and freshly ground pepper, to taste

1 bouquet garni consisting of 4 large sprigs parsley, 2 sprigs fresh thyme, and 1 bay leaf, tied together with string

2 large leeks, white parts only, cut into 4 pieces, each about 2 inches long

1 medium celery root, trimmed and cut into 4-6 pieces, each 2 inches long

2 large carrots, trimmed and cut into 4-6 pieces, each 2 inches long

4 new small white turnips, peeled, with green stems left on

½ cup shelled fresh peas

1 cup french beans or haricots verts, stems removed

One sheet fresh or frozen thawed store-bought puff pastry, approximately 12 x 12 inches, ¼ inch thick

1 egg yolk beaten with 1 tablespoon water, to brush on pastry

1. Preheat the oven to 350° F.

2. Carefully loosen the skin around the breast and legs of the chicken with your fingers. Insert the truffle slices between the skin and the meat—2 on each breast and 1 on each leg.

3. Season the cavity of the chicken with salt and pepper. Tuck the wings under the chicken and place it on its back in the bottom of the tureen. Add the bouquet garni. Arrange all the vegetables over the chicken and season with salt and pepper.

4. Lay the puff pastry over the tureen and press the edges all around to seal tightly. There should be a 2-inch lip extending over the edge.

5. Brush the top and edges evenly with the egg yolk mixture.

6. Place the tureen in the lower half of the oven and cook for 1¼ hours, rotating occasionally for even cooking, or until the top is nicely browned.

7. To serve, cut the pastry all around the rim and set aside. Remove the chicken, carve, and place the chicken on serving plates with the vegetables and juices. Cut the puff pastry into wedges and place a wedge on top of each serving.

BLACK SEA BASS WITH A POTATO CRUST AND A LIGHT VINAIGRETTE

YIELD: 4 SERVINGS

In this recipe, thinly cut potatoes are placed on the fish fillets to resemble scales. The fillets are cooked until the potato scales are lightly browned and crunchy, allowing the fish to stay moist inside. Paul makes this low-fat dish with red mullet (rouget), a fish that is very difficult to obtain in the United States, and serves it as an appetizer at his three-star restaurant, near Lyon. I make it here using Black Sea Bass. Serve this dish with sautéed spinach or a mixed green salad.

2 large Idaho potatoes, peeled
1 tablespoon melted butter
4 4-ounce fillets of black sea bass, red snapper, or rock-fish, with skin or without
Salt and freshly ground pepper, to taste
1 egg yolk lightly beaten with 2 tablespoons water
2 tablespoons fresh lemon juice
¼ cup coarsely chopped fresh chervil or fresh parsley
½ cup peeled, seeded, and diced tomatoes
5 tablespoons extra-virgin olive oil
¼ cup chopped chives

1. Cut the potatoes into ⅛-inch slices or thinner. Place them on a flat surface and cut into uniform rounds using a ¾-inch round metal cutter. Cut as many rounds as possible—they will be used to simulate the scales of a fish. There should be 20-24 rounds for each fillet. In a saucepan, bring enough water to a boil and add the potato slices. Blanch for 10 seconds. Drain immediately and let cool. Dip the potato slices into the melted butter, then set them aside and keep lukewarm.

2. Lay the 4 fish fillets on a flat surface. Season with salt and pepper. Brush the tops with the egg yolk mixture. Lay the potato slices on each fillet, overlapping each one with the next one. Place in the refrigerator for 10 minutes to harden the butter and fix the scales together.

3. Meanwhile place the lemon juice, chervil, tomatoes, and 4 tablespoons olive oil in a small mixing bowl and season with salt and pepper. Blend well with a wire whisk and let vinaigrette stand briefly.

4. Over medium-high heat, heat the remaining 1 tablespoon olive oil in a nonstick skillet that will hold the fillets in one layer. Add the fillets, potato side down. Cook until the potatoes are lightly browned, about 5 minutes. Carefully turn the fillets and cook, basting often, about 4 more minutes. Take care not to overcook.

5. To serve, divide the vinaigrette over each plate. Place each fillet in the center with the potato side up. Sprinkle with the chopped chives and serve immediately.

MACKEREL FILLETS IN WHITE WINE

YIELD: 10 SERVINGS

This is one of my favorite luncheon dishes. My grand-mother and mother used to make it for me when I was a child and the recipe hasn't changed over the years. I like to prepare this dish in large quantities. Its flavor improves with time. Plan to make it at least a day before serving. It remains good for sev-eral more days. This dish can also be made with other fish fillets such as small red snapper, or shrimp, but the cooking time for the shrimp will be less— about 5 minutes in the oven.

2 tablespoons olive oil

1 cup thinly sliced white onion

¼ cup thinly sliced carrots

2 finely minced garlic cloves

Salt and freshly ground pepper, to taste

2 tablespoons white wine vinegar

1½ cups dry white wine

3 whole cloves

4 sprigs fresh thyme

1 bay leaf

10 mackerel fillets, skinless if desired

10 thin lemon slices, seeded

3 tablespoons fresh lemon juice

1. Preheat the oven to 400° F.

2. Heat 1 tablespoon of the oil in a medium saucepan, add the onion, and cook over medium-high heat, stirring, until wilted. Add the carrots, garlic, salt and pepper, vinegar, white wine, cloves, thyme, and bay leaf. Lower the heat and simmer for 10 minutes.

3. Select a baking dish large enough to hold the mackerel in one layer. Rub the bottom of the dish with the remaining olive oil and sprinkle lightly with salt and pepper. Arrange the mackerel side by side in the dish. Place the lemon slices over the fish and sprinkle with the lemon juice. Sprinkle salt and pepper lightly over all.

4. Pour the wine sauce over the fish evenly. Cover with waxed paper cut to fit the baking dish and bake for 10-15 minutes, just until the fish flakes evenly when tested with a fork. The time will depend on the thickness of the fish.

5. Remove from the oven, let cool, and place in refrigerator. Serve cold.

LEEKS VINAIGRETTE

YIELD: 4 SERVINGS

The leek, a member of the onion family, is a mainstay of the European diet. Leeks are found in soups and salads and are served as accompaniments to other dishes. This recipe will keep for several days under refrigeration and can be served as an appetizer or luncheon dish.

4 large, unblemished leeks or 8 small ones, about 2 pounds
Salt, to taste
1 tablespoon Dijon mustard
2 tablespoons red wine vinegar
2 tablespoons finely chopped shallots
Freshly ground pepper, to taste
2 tablespoons corn oil
2 tablespoons olive oil
2 tablespoons finely chopped parsley

1. Trim off the root ends of the leeks but leave the bases solid and intact. Trim off the green tops crosswise, leaving a base 5-7 inches long. The trimmed weight should be about 1¼ pounds.

2. Using a sharp knife, split the leeks in half lengthwise starting about 3 inches from the stem end and cutting through the leaves. Rinse the leeks well under cold running water, being careful to remove the dirt between the leaves. Tie the leeks together in 2 bunches with string. Place the leeks in a pan, add cold water to cover, and season with salt. Bring to a boil and simmer 10-15 minutes, or until done. You can test for doneness by piercing the base with a knife. The cooking time of the leeks will vary depending on the size and age of the leeks. Take care never to overcook leeks or they will be mushy. Drain the leeks thoroughly and let stand until cool enough to handle. Press them between your hands to extract excess liquid. Untie.

3. Split the leeks the remaining way lengthwise, then in half crosswise. Arrange them neatly on a serving dish.

4. Place the mustard, vinegar, shallots, and salt and pepper in a small bowl. Beat vigorously with a wire whisk. Gradually add the oils, beating constantly, as if you were making mayonnaise. It should become very thick.

5. Spoon the sauce over the leeks and sprinkle with parsley.

NOTE: The cooking liquid of the leeks can be saved and used as a base for soup or other dishes, and the remaining green leaves can be used to flavor stock or broth.

POTATO–GOAT CHEESE QUICHE

YIELD: 6-8 SERVINGS

This Potato–Goat Cheese Quiche is a variation of the traditional quiche made with Gruyère or Comté. To lower the fat content I use plain low-fat yogurt instead of milk and heavy cream. I also use one egg instead of four. This quiche can be served as an appetizer or for a luncheon with a mixed green salad.

1½ pounds baby red potatoes or any small new potatoes
Salt, to taste
2 garlic cloves, peeled
4 ounces fresh goat cheese
2 tablespoons finely chopped scallions
1 whole egg, lightly beaten
2 cup drained plain low-fat yogurt
Freshly ground pepper, to taste
⅛ teaspoon freshly grated nutmeg
Pinch of cayenne pepper
Cheese Pastry Dough (see following page)
2 tablespoons grated Parmesan or Gruyère cheese

1.   Preheat the oven to 350° F.

2.   Wash the potatoes and place them in a small saucepan with water to cover. Add salt. Bring to a boil and cook for about 15 minutes, or until they are done. Let cool, peel, and cut them (carefully so as to not break them) into ¼-inch or smaller slices.

3.   Meanwhile, as the potatoes cook, add the garlic to the pot of simmering water and cook for 2 minutes. Remove and split the cloves in half, removing any green core, and chop finely.

4.   In a mixing bowl, crush the goat cheese with a fork until smooth. Add the garlic, scallions, and egg and blend well. Add the yogurt, salt, pepper, nutmeg, and cayenne. Blend well with a wire whisk until smooth.

5.   Line a 9- or 10-inch quiche pan with the pastry dough. Arrange the potato slices carefully in a circular manner, overlapping to cover the bottom of the quiche pan. Pour the goat cheese mixture over the potatoes and sprinkle with the Parmesan cheese.

6.   Put the quiche on a baking sheet and place on the bottom rack of the oven. Bake for 40 minutes, turning several times to cook evenly. It should be lightly browned. Remove and serve warm.

CHEESE PASTRY DOUGH

YIELD: ONE 9- TO
10-INCH PASTRY SHELL
OR 6 INDIVIDUAL
3-INCH SHELLS

This Cheese Pastry Dough is quick to assemble and can be used to make any kind of vegetable or meat quiche.

1 ½ cups all-purpose flour
3 tablespoons olive oil
Salt, to taste
¼ cup grated Gruyère or Cheddar cheese

1. Place the flour, olive oil, 1 tablespoon cold water, salt, and cheese in a food processor and blend until a ball is formed. You may have to add an additional tablespoon of water to moisten the dough.

2. Remove the dough and shape it into a ball. Chill in the refrigerator for 10 minutes.

3. Transfer the ball of dough to a floured surface and flatten it slightly with the palm of your hand. Sprinkle the ball lightly with flour and roll out the dough evenly, giving it a quarter-turn after each roll. The dough should be rolled to about ⅛-inch thickness.

4. Line a pie or quiche pan with the pastry. Pastry shell is ready to be filled.

SPINACH WITH NUTMEG

YIELD: 4 SERVINGS

Spinach is rich in iron and vitamins and it cooks quickly.

1 pound spinach leaves or a 10-ounce package fresh spinach
2 tablespoons butter
Salt, to taste (optional)
Freshly ground pepper, to taste
¼ teaspoon freshly grated nutmeg

1. Wash the spinach and drain well. Cut away and discard any tough spinach stems and blemished leaves.

2. Heat the butter in a large skillet over medium-high heat and add the spinach, salt, pepper, and nutmeg. Stir as the spinach wilts. Cook until the spinach is totally wilted, 3-4 minutes. Remove from the heat and serve.

WATERCRESS AND ENDIVE SALAD WITH WALNUTS

—

YIELD: 4 SERVINGS

I like the combination of watercress and endive because of contrasts in color, shape, and texture. The walnuts add a crunchy quality to this salad.

1 large bunch watercress
2 large Belgian endive
1 tablespoon Dijon mustard
1 tablespooon red wine vinegar
Salt and freshly ground pepper, to taste
3 tablespoons olive oil
½ cup thinly sliced red onion
¼ cup broken walnuts
2 tablespoons fresh chervil or parsley

1. Cut off the tough stems of the watercress and discard. Cut off the ends of the endive and cut the endive into bite-size pieces. Rinse the watercress and endive and dry well.

2. In a salad bowl, combine the mustard, vinegar, and salt and pepper and blend well with a wire whisk. Add the oil slowly until blended.

3. Add the watercress, endive, red onion, and walnuts. Toss well and sprinkle with chervil or parsley.

BANANA SHERBET WITH YOGURT AND STRAWBERRY SAUCE

YIELD: 4 SERVINGS

This dessert can be made ahead of time. However, it is important to stir the sherbet occasionally so that it does not freeze solid. If it does, thaw it briefly and re-mix it by hand. Other fresh fruit, such as raspberries or blackberries, can be substituted for the strawberries. This strawberry sauce can also be used as a dessert sauce over ice cream, or you can mix it with fresh fruit or serve it pooled under a slice of cake on a plate.

3 ripe but firm bananas
5 tablespoons sugar
1 cup plain low-fat yogurt
Fresh strawberries, for garnish
Fresh mint leaves, for garnish

1. Peel the bananas, cut them into ¼-inch slices, and place them on a platter in a single layer. Cover with plastic wrap and place in the freezer for 4-5 hours or more.

2. Place the frozen banana slices in a food processor, add the sugar, and blend at high speed for about 10 seconds. Add the yogurt and continue blending at high speed until of a fine and smooth consistency. The whole process should take no more than 40 seconds. Remove, place in a bowl, and put in the freezer. Stir occasionally with a rubber spatula. Keep in freezer until ready to serve.

3. To assemble, place 1 ball of banana sherbet in the center of each of 4 cold plates. Place the Strawberry Sauce around and place fresh strawberries over the sherbet, with a few fresh mint leaves on the side or on the sherbet for garnish.

STRAWBERRY SAUCE

1 pint fresh strawberries
½ cup sugar
2 tablespoons Grand Marnier or liqueur of your choice

1. Remove the hulls from the strawberries. Combine the strawberries, sugar, and Grand Marnier in a food processor until smooth. If desired, push through a sieve to remove the seeds. Transfer to a covered container and store in refrigerator until ready to use.

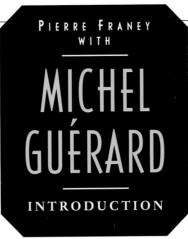

PIERRE FRANEY
WITH

MICHEL GUÉRARD

INTRODUCTION

Right in the heart of France's southwest is an area called "les Landes," south of the city of Bordeaux. It is a peaceful region, made up of sand dunes along the Atlantic coast, marshes, and pine forests farther east. It serves as a home to many different kinds of small birds—thrushes, doves, woodcock, and quail. Gastronomically speaking, southwest France is also known for its foie gras, duck, and Armagnac.

In the quiet town of Eugénie-les-Bains sits the luxurious country inn, spa, and dining rooms of Michel Guérard. The town is named after Empress Eugénie of the

RIGHT: *Pierre and his wife, Betty, enjoy a restful moment in the garden of les Pres d'Eugénie.*
OPPOSITE: *The entrance to the dining rooms of Michel Guérard.*

Second Empire, who came here frequently to partake of its soothing waters. Michel and his wife, Christine, have lived here for more than twenty years, making it a sought-after vacation destination for people from all over the world. Michel became famous with his "cuisine minceur" (lean cuisine), by using imaginative ways of cooking low-fat and low-calorie dishes while staying within the tradition of French cooking. For example, he replaces heavy cream with a combination of chicken broth and low-fat milk. And he steams meats and vegetables and takes the time to reduce his sauces to bring out strong and intense flavors without added fat. He believes in retaining purity of flavor and, when combining different ingredients, takes care to bring harmony to the palate. A recent typical "Grande Cuisine Minceur" menu at his restaurant offered a 480-calorie lunch and a 300-calorie dinner.

Of course, Michel was trained in the classical French method and, like many European chefs, was greatly influenced by the cooking of his grandmother and mother. He was born just north of Paris and apprenticed there as a young man. Michel became pastry chef at the Hotel Crillon in Paris, then

OPPOSITE AND RIGHT: *La Ferme aux Grives, Guérard's country inn, features a rustic and inviting atmosphere that includes stone walls decorated with an assortment of bird cages in the dining room and an open hearth in the kitchen.*
OVERLEAF: *Michel and Pierre dine at La Ferme aux Grives.*

opened a very successful bistro on the outskirts of the city. When his restaurant was torn down to make way for a new highway, he and his wife took off for the southwest of France and have been there ever since.

Although he is known for his "cuisine minceur," his real love is his "cuisine gourmande," which—though more caloric—retains Michel's refined manner and concern for purity of flavor, light sauces, and the right combination of foods. He confided in me that he eats his "cuisine minceur" only once a week.

My visit with him was very rewarding, and Michel took good care of me. We cooked together in the morning and then sat down to lunch in his main dining room. I ate from his "cuisine minceur" menu while he ate from his "cuisine gourmande" menu! In the late afternoon, I went to the

health spa and was given a mud bath. It was the first mud bath I'd ever had, and it worked wonders on a pinched nerve.

Michel was happy to share with me two of his "cuisine minceur" recipes, a Tomato Tart and an Apple-Lime Soufflé (see pages 25 and 26). They are light to eat and simple to make.

FROM MICHEL GUÉRARD

TOMATO TART

❦

APPLE-LIME SOUFFLÉ

FROM PIERRE FRANEY

STEAMED SALMON FILLETS
WITH FENNEL AND YOGURT SAUCE

❦

STEAMED PARSLEYED POTATOES
WITH CUCUMBERS

❦

VEGETABLE SOUP RAPHAELLE

❦

BROILED MAHIMAHI
IN ESCABÈCHE SAUCE

❦

BAKED EGGS RATATOUILLE

TOMATO TART

YIELD: 4 SERVINGS

This tomato tart is served as a first course on Michel Guérard's "cuisine minceur" menu at his three-star restaurant. You'll see that he saves the core and stem of the tomato to use as part of the presentation on the plate. And the seeds are carefully removed with tweezers to retain the shape of the tomato, although you don't have to do that at home.

12 ounces fresh or frozen store-bought puff pastry

4 tablespoons olive oil

1 tablespoon chopped fresh basil

8 ripe plum tomatoes (4 ounces each), preferably with stem and a few leaves attached, cored (reserve core with stem and leaves for garnish)

3 tablespoons tomato paste

Salt and freshly ground pepper, to taste

Tabasco sauce (optional)

1 teaspoon NutraSweet or 2 teaspoons sugar

1 tablespoon fresh thyme leaves, or 1 teaspoon dried

8 basil leaves, for garnish

1. Preheat the oven to 425° F.

2. Roll out the puff pastry to an ⅛-inch thickness. Lay an 8-inch flan ring over the pastry and cut 4 circles, each 8 inches in diameter.

3. Brush a large baking sheet lightly with 1 tablespoon olive oil and place the pastry circles on the sheet, leaving at least 2 inches between each one. Set aside in a cool place.

4. In a small bowl, combine the remaining 3 tablespoons olive oil and the chopped basil. Blend well and set aside.

5. Bring a large saucepan of water to a boil. Add the cored tomatoes and blanch for about 10 seconds. Drain, cool, and peel. Slice tomatoes evenly into rounds ¼-inch thick. Remove the seeds by gently pushing with fingers (or picking out with a tweezer), leaving the flesh intact.

6. In a small bowl, combine the tomato paste with half the olive oil mixture.

7. Prick the pastry circles all over with a fork, then spread the tomato paste–olive oil mixture evenly over each circle in a thin layer, leaving a clean edge of about ¼ inch.

8. Lay the tomato slices on the pastry to cover the tomato paste–olive oil. Fill in the tomato centers with remaining slices to create a solid layer.

9. Season with salt and pepper, and sprinkle lightly with Tabasco, if desired. Sprinkle lightly with NutraSweet and fresh thyme leaves.

10. Place the tarts in the oven for 15 minutes. Remove from the oven and brush with any remaining basil–olive oil mixture. Garnish with the tomato cores and fresh basil. Serve immediately.

APPLE-LIME SOUFFLÉ

YIELD: 4 SERVINGS

Michel serves this dessert on his "cuisine minceur" menu at his three-star restaurant. It is sweetened with NutraSweet, an artificial sweetener. If you prefer, sugar can be substituted.

4 teaspoons butter, softened

Juice and zest of 1 lime

3 tablespoons NutraSweet or ½ cup sugar, mixed with 1 cup water

2 large Golden Delicious apples with stems, unpeeled, quartered

2 egg yolks

10 egg whites

Salt

2 teaspoons confectioners' sugar

1. Preheat the oven to 400° F.

2. Brush four 2-cup soufflé molds with the softened butter. Be sure the bottom and edges are well coated. Refrigerate until ready to use.

3. Blanch the lime zest in boiling water and strain; repeat 2 more times, straining each time. Place the NutraSweet mixture in saucepan and add the blanched zest. Simmer 30 minutes, then remove. Drain, reserving the syrup, and finely chop. (Recipe can be done ahead of time up to this point.)

4. In a small saucepan, combine the apples and ¼ cup water or more to cover. Bring to a boil, cover, and simmer 10 minutes. Uncover, raise heat, and boil to reduce any excess moisture; the apples should be very soft, without too much moisture. Let cool. Transfer to a food processor and puree. Push puree through a medium strainer to remove skin, stems, and seeds.

5. Place strained apple puree in a large mixing bowl. Add the lime zest and juice and the egg yolks and mix well.

6. Place the egg whites in a large mixing bowl. Add a pinch of salt and begin to beat with a wire whisk. As the whites form soft peaks, gradually add the NutraSweet syrup. Do not overbeat.

7. Add one-third of the egg whites to the apple puree and fold in. Then add the reserved remaining whites and fold gently until combined thoroughly.

8. Spoon equal amounts of the mixture into the prepared molds. The mixture should reach ¼ inch below rim. Run your thumb around the top of each rim to allow for expansion. Place the dishes on a baking sheet and put on the lower rack of the oven. Bake for about 8 minutes or until the soufflés have risen about 1 inch over the top and tops are lightly brown.

9. Remove the soufflés from the oven and sprinkle with confectioners' sugar. Serve immediately.

STEAMED SALMON FILLETS WITH FENNEL AND YOGURT SAUCE

YIELD: 4 SERVINGS

No oil or butter is used to cook this fish. You can make this preparation using any firm fish, such as striped bass, tilefish, red snapper, or halibut. The Fennel and Yogurt Sauce keeps the fat content low. Ten years ago, I would have made it with cream and butter. It can be served with seafood or poultry. The basic sauce can be made ahead of time, but the yogurt should not be added until you are ready to serve. If adding later, blend the sauce with a wire whisk.

¼ cup white wine vinegar
4 firm skinless salmon fillets (about 6 ounces each)
Salt and freshly ground pepper, to taste
½ teaspoon ground coriander
4 sprigs fresh rosemary or dill

1. Fill the bottom of a steamer about half full with water and add the vinegar. Place the fish fillets on the rack of the steamer. Add salt and pepper, then sprinkle each fillet with coriander. Place 1 sprig rosemary or dill on top of each fillet. Cover, bring to a boil, and steam 5-6 minutes or until the fish is tender when pierced with the tip of a knife and has lost its raw look.

2. Place the fish fillets on warm serving plates, then spoon warm Fennel and Yogurt Sauce over and around them. (Do not remove the rosemary.)

FENNEL AND YOGURT SAUCE

2 tablespoons olive oil
1 fennel bulb, trimmed and thinly sliced (about 1 cup)
2 tablespoons sliced shallots
1 tablespoon chopped garlic
4 tablespoons white wine vinegar
¾ cup fresh or canned chicken broth
Dash of Tabasco sauce
1 teaspoon ground coriander
1 teaspoon fresh thyme leaves, or ¼ teaspoon dried
¼ cup drained plain low-fat yogurt
Salt and freshly ground pepper, to taste

1. Heat the olive oil in a small saucepan over medium-high heat and add the fennel, shallots, and garlic. Cook, stirring, until wilted, about 5 minutes.

2. Add the vinegar, stir, and cook for 1 minute. Add the chicken broth, Tabasco, coriander, and thyme. Reduce heat and simmer for about 15 minutes.

3. Transfer to a high-speed food processor or blender and blend to a fine texture. Add the yogurt and blend again for 15 seconds. Season with salt and pepper. Serve warm; if reheated, be sure not to boil.

STEAMED PARSLEYED POTATOES WITH CUCUMBERS

YIELD: 4 SERVINGS

Cucumbers, which are fat-free but mostly water, are rather tasteless on their own. It is unusual to cook cucumbers, but they make a delicious side dish if combined with potatoes. When I was a chef at Le Pavillon in New York City, we served this with poached fish and fish mousse.

8 small red-skinned potatoes (about ¾ pound)
2 large firm cucumbers
1 tablespoon olive oil
2 tablespoons chopped flat-leaf parsley
Salt and freshly ground pepper, to taste
Juice of ½ lemon

1.   Using a sharp knife, cut the potatoes in half and peel some skin off, leaving a band in the center of each for color.

2.   Trim off the ends of the cucumbers and remove the peel. Cut them into 2-inch rounds. Quarter each slice lengthwise and remove the seeds.

3.   Place the potatoes on the rack of a steamer over boiling water and steam for 10 minutes. Add the cucumbers and steam for 3 minutes more. Do not overcook.

4.   Heat the oil in a large saucepan and add the potatoes, cucumbers, parsley, salt, pepper, and lemon juice. Toss, heat for 30 seconds, and serve.

A table setting in the dining room at La Ferme aux Grives.

VEGETABLE SOUP RAPHAELLE

YIELD: 8-10 SERVINGS

I created this recipe on the day my grand-daughter Raphaelle was born. Upon returning to my son's home that evening, I opened the refrigerator and made a soup with what I found. We also cracked open a bottle of Champagne to celebrate the big event. Any other vegetables may be added, such as cauliflower, green beans, peas, or whatever is in your refrigerator!

2 tablespoons olive oil
1 cup chopped onion
1 garlic clove, finely chopped
2 cups coarsely sliced carrots
3 large Idaho potatoes, cut into large cubes (about 4 cups)
3 celery stalks
⅛ teaspoon hot red pepper flakes
Salt and freshly ground pepper, to taste
4 cups fresh or canned chicken broth
Pinch of dried thyme or a few sprigs fresh thyme
½ cup drained plain low-fat yogurt
2 tablespoons chopped parsley

1. Place the olive oil in a large saucepan, add the onion, and cook over medium heat until wilted. Add the garlic, carrots, potatoes, celery, red pepper flakes, salt, and pepper. Cook a few minutes, then add the broth, 4 cups water, and the thyme. Reduce the heat and simmer for 30 minutes.

2. Push the soup mixture through a food mill or blend in a food processor. Return to the saucepan and add the yogurt. Heat until hot—do not boil. Sprinkle with parsley and serve.

BROILED MAHIMAHI IN ESCABÈCHE SAUCE

YIELD: 4 SERVINGS

Escabèche is a spicy, flavorful sauce of Spanish origin, often used in French cooking. It can be served warm or cold and goes well with fish, shellfish, and broiled or roasted meats.

2 tablespoons olive oil

4 mahimahi steaks (4-5 ounces each), skinless and boneless

Salt and freshly ground pepper, to taste

4 tablespoons chopped chives

1. Preheat a grill or broiler until very hot.

2. Brush oil over the steaks and season with salt and pepper. Marinate about 15 minutes at room temperature.

3. While the fish is marinating, make the sauce below.

4. Grill or broil the fish 2-3 minutes on each side or until done. (Test for doneness by inserting the sharp point of a paring knife in center of fish.) Remove and pour sauce over fish. Sprinkle with chopped chives.

ESCABÈCHE SAUCE

2 tablespoons olive oil

1 large red bell pepper, cored, seeded, and diced in ¼-inch cubes

2 tablespoons chopped shallots

Salt and freshly ground pepper, to taste

4 tablespoons capers

2 tablespoons red wine vinegar

¼ teaspoon Tabasco sauce, or ¼ teaspoon hot red pepper flakes

1. Heat the oil in a small saucepan. Add the red pepper, shallots, salt, and pepper and sauté, stirring, over medium-high heat for 3 minutes. Add the capers, vinegar, and Tabasco and cook several minutes more. Keep warm.

BAKED EGGS RATATOUILLE

YIELD: 4 SERVINGS

This was one of my favorite dishes when I was growing up in Burgundy. My mother would serve this to my brothers and me along with a crusty loaf of French bread. I love to eat eggs with the white firm and the yellow runny. But in these days of possible salmonella in eggs, you may want to cook them thoroughly.

2 tablespoons olive oil

2 medium eggplants (about 1 pound total weight), cored, peeled, and cut into ½-inch cubes

2 small zucchini (about 1 pound), ends trimmed and cut into ½-inch cubes

1 medium green bell pepper, cored, seeded and cut into ½-inch cubes

1 medium red bell pepper, cored, seeded, and cut into ½-inch cubes

1 cup coarsely chopped onion

1 tablespoon finely chopped garlic

2 cups cored and diced ripe plum tomatoes

3 tablespoons tomato paste

1 bay leaf

2 sprigs fresh thyme, or ½ teaspoon dried

⅛ teaspoon hot red pepper flakes

Salt and freshly ground pepper, to taste

8 large eggs

¼ cup freshly grated pecorino or Parmesan cheese

1.   Preheat the oven to 400° F.

2.   In a heavy ovenproof casserole or skillet, heat the oil over medium-high heat. When very hot, add the eggplant and zucchini and cook, stirring, about 2 minutes. Add the green and red peppers and onion and cook, stirring, for about 6 minutes. Add the garlic and stir.

3.   Add the tomatoes, tomato paste, bay leaf, thyme, red pepper flakes, salt, and pepper. Bring to a boil, stirring. Cover and place the casserole in the oven; bake for 20 minutes.

4.   Pour the vegetable mixture into a baking dish that measures 8½ x 13½ x 2 inches. Smooth over the top. Make 8 indentations in the center of the ratatouille and break 1 egg into each opening.

5.   Sprinkle the cheese evenly over the surface of the dish. Place in the oven and bake 10 minutes. (Cook two minutes longer if you prefer your egg yolks to be thoroughly cooked.) Serve immediately.

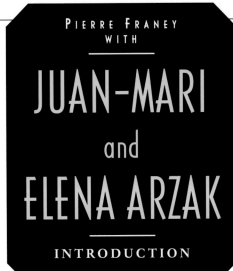

JUAN-MARI
and
ELENA ARZAK

INTRODUCTION

O n the northern coast of Spain, at the edge of a scallop-shaped bay, sits the picturesque fishing port of San Sebastián. It is one of the gastronomic centers of Spain, with a cuisine that is based on a combination of Basque, Spanish, and French influences. Throughout the year, fishing boats bring in their bountiful catches, including hake, sardines, dorade (bream), cod, tuna, anchovy, and squid. While I was visiting, the anchovy were running. The fishermen catch them in large nets and put them in holding tanks on board their boats. The live anchovies are then brought directly to the local fish factories, where they are salted and marinated in olive oil, then canned. Local residents do their own preserving and eat anchovies, a local specialty, throughout the year.

San Sebastián is a city full of restaurants, ranging from tapas bars to family-run seafood restaurants to private eating clubs. Everywhere I walked I was tempted by the most wonderful-sounding menus. I had a delicious lunch in a restaurant on the port. A giant turbot was cooked on an open charcoal grill and basted with a mixture of lemon juice, vinegar, olive oil, and sea salt. Seared at a high temperature, the fish was so moist and tender, it was simply served with its own cooking juices.

A typical street front in a coastal village near San Sebastián.

On a busy street in the heart of San Sebastián, I visited Juan-Mari Arzak, whose restaurant, Arzak, is considered one of the best in Spain. It is a small, unassuming spot specializing in fresh fish. The decor is simple and the waitresses are dressed very primly, in black dresses with white starched collars. Juan-Mari and his daughter, Elena, are the chefs in a kitchen with a small staff. The restaurant was started about one hundred years ago by Juan-Mari's father. Back then it was a modest country bistro whose clientele were local residents.

Over the years, Juan-Mari has brought worldwide recognition to his restaurant by cooking in a style of his own, with prominent Basque and French accents. Elena trained with several French chefs before joining her father. They sincerely believe that fresh ingredients are the key to a good cuisine, and the natural flavors of fresh ingredients eliminate the need to use a lot of fat. Cooking with only local products, their menu varies throughout the year depending on what is in season. The dominance of fish on the menu makes for meals that are light and low in fat. Juan-Mari is a true "man about town" who knows many other restaurateurs and producers in San Sebastián. As I walked through the city streets with him, he was constantly greeted by shopkeepers, merchants, and owners of markets. He has strong ties with local farmers and producers, who make daily deliveries directly to his restaurant, bringing the choicest of vegetables, fruit, fish, and meats. One of the places we visited together was a huge market in a block-long building with the most amazing variety of fish from the

LEFT: *Fresh anchovies, a local favorite, are sold in San Sebastián's fish market.*
OPPOSITE: *Pierre with Elena and Juan-Mari Arzak in front of their restaurant.*
OVERLEAF: *Local fishing boats moored in the picturesque harbor at San Sebastián.*

Atlantic Ocean as well as from the Mediterranean Sea. What a wonderful place for any chef or home cook to come to each day to choose from the morning's catch!

Back in their kitchen, Juan-Mari and Elena prepared some delightful dishes for me, including langoustine cooked with herbs and black caraway seeds, shrimp with fried leeks, and Fillet of Hake with Clams in Green Sauce (see page 40). The hake and clams are cooked in water seasoned with garlic and parsley. It is a tasty and simple dish to make, but it requires a bit of loving care, as you stand by the stove and constantly baste the fish in its cooking broth.

From Juan-Mari Arzak

Fillet of Hake with Clams in Green Sauce

❧

Fresh Figs with Blackberries and Currant Jelly

From Pierre Franey

Braised Fennel

❧

Basque Fish Stew

❧

Rice Pilaf with Zucchini and Red Peppers

❧

Apple Aïoli

❧

Seafood Salad

❧

Ginger Vinaigrette

❧

Poached Pears in Port Wine

❧

Bay Scallops in Shallot Sauce

FILLET OF HAKE WITH CLAMS IN GREEN SAUCE

—

YIELD: 4 SERVINGS

This recipe requires a lot of attention because all the cooking is done on top of the stove. It is important to baste the fish constantly with the cooking broth and turn the clams so that they open and cook evenly. The green sauce gets its color from parsley. If you can't find hake, you can substitute cod.

4 tablespoons olive oil

4 teaspoons chopped garlic

4 tablespoons chopped flat-leaf parsley

24 littleneck clams, all the same size (mussels can be used if clams are not available), scrubbed well

4 5-ounce center-cut hake fillets, skin on, ½ inch thick

Sea salt and freshly ground pepper, to taste

4 tablespoons all-purpose flour

1. Heat the oil over low heat in a large, heavy-gauge 10- to 12-inch nonstick skillet. Add the garlic and 1 tablespoon of parsley and stir until wilted.

2. Place the clams at the outside edge of the skillet. Season the fish with salt and pepper on both sides and place in the center of the skillet skin side up. Cook very slowly for a few minutes. Sprinkle flour in the skillet between the fish and gradually add 2 cups water, stirring constantly to blend so that no lumps are formed. Turn the fish and the clams and continue cooking slowly, taking care not to let liquid boil. The total cooking time is approximately 10 minutes. To help with the cooking, you must baste continually. Check the sauce; if it is too thick, thin it with a little more water. Add 1 tablespoon parsley and baste the fish with the sauce.

3. As soon as the clams open, remove them from the skillet and place them around the edges of 4 serving plates. Discard any clams that do not open. Check the fish for doneness with the tip of a small paring knife by inserting it into the center of the fish. Be careful not to overcook. Place a fish fillet in the center of each plate and pour some of the sauce over the top. Garnish each plate with the remaining 2 tablespoons parsley.

FRESH FIGS WITH BLACKBERRIES AND CURRANT JELLY

YIELD: 4 SERVINGS

This simple dessert must be made with fresh figs, which are available in summer and early fall. Check for freshness and ripeness—the cut stems should not be dried out and the figs should be unblemished and soft when squeezed gently.

1½ cups plain low-fat yogurt
¼ cup whole milk
1 cup currant jelly, at room temperature
2 cups blackberries or raspberries
12 large ripe figs

1. In a medium mixing bowl, combine the yogurt and milk. Add ½ cup currant jelly and blend gently. Set aside.

2. Carefully combine the remaining ½ cup of currant jelly with the blackberries. Set aside.

3. Cut each fig into quarters starting at the blossom end, taking care not to cut all the way through. Spread open slightly so the fig resembles a blossom.

4. Drop one-fourth of the yogurt mixture onto the center of each of the 4 serving plates. Place 3 opened figs over the yogurt and scatter the blackberries over and around the figs before serving.

BRAISED FENNEL

—

YIELD: 4-8 SERVINGS

Fennel is a very popular vegetable in Spain, Italy, and France, but is not yet well known in much of the United States. Fennel has the texture of celery, with a delicate, sweet licorice taste. It is excellent when braised, as in this recipe, or can be chopped raw and added to a salad. The "heart" or center of the fennel is very tender. In fact, all parts of the fennel bulb are edible, including the delicate green leaves, which can be used as a garnish.

4 fresh unblemished fennel bulbs
1 tablespoon olive oil
1 tablespoon fresh lemon juice
6 coriander seeds
2 sprigs fresh thyme, or ½ teaspoon dried
1 bay leaf
Salt and freshly ground pepper, to taste

1. Cut off the tops of the fennel, and remove any outer stalks that may be discolored. Trim the base. Wash well, then cut each in half lengthwise.

2. Place the fennel in one layer in a large pan with a tight-fitting lid. Add 2 cups water, the olive oil, lemon juice, coriander seeds, thyme, bay leaf, salt, and pepper. Bring to a boil, cover, and simmer until tender, 20-25 minutes. Remove the thyme sprigs and bay leaf, and serve.

NOTE: As a variation, place some of the cooking liquid in the bottom of the pan, add the cooked fennel, and sprinkle on 4 tablespoons of pecorino, Parmesan, or Gruyère cheese. Place under the broiler until lightly browned, about 3 minutes.

BASQUE FISH STEW

YIELD: 4-6 SERVINGS

This recipe can be made in advance. Clean and prepare the seafood and make the base with the vegetables, but add the seafood just before serving so you don't overcook it.

1 pound skinless striped bass or monkfish fillets

1 pound skinless red snapper fillets, or any other white-fleshed firm fish

½ pound raw medium shrimp

1 pound mussels or clams

2 tablespoons olive oil

1½ cups finely chopped onion

1 cup finely diced celery

1 cup finely diced green bell pepper

1 cup dry white wine

3 cups canned crushed tomatoes

1 bay leaf

2 sprigs fresh thyme, or ½ teaspoon dried

¼ teaspoon hot red pepper flakes

Salt and freshly ground pepper, to taste

1 tablespoon finely chopped garlic

¼ cup finely chopped flat-leaf parsley

1. Cut the fish into 1½-inch cubes and set aside. Shell and devein the shrimp and set aside. Scrub the mussels well, remove the beards, and set aside.

2. Heat the olive oil in a large, deep pot over medium-high heat, add the onion, and cook, stirring, until wilted. Add the celery and green pepper, and cook, stirring, about 5 minutes. Raise the heat and cook down the liquid about 1 minute, then add the wine, tomatoes, bay leaf, thyme, red pepper flakes, salt, and pepper. Bring to a boil, then reduce heat and simmer for 12 minutes.

3. Add the fish cubes and mussels to the pot, blend well, and cook over high heat for 3 minutes. Add the shrimp, immersing them in the sauce, and let cook for 1 minute. Sprinkle with garlic and parsley, stir, and simmer about 3 minutes longer. Serve with Apple Aïoli (see page 45) and Garlic Croutons (see page 98).

RICE PILAF WITH ZUCCHINI AND RED PEPPERS

YIELD: 4 SERVINGS

You must use converted rice to make this pilaf. The grains of converted rice are harder and more compact, and they will remain separate.

1 tablespoon olive oil

½ cup finely chopped onion

2 teaspoons finely chopped garlic

2 small zucchini (about ½ pound), trimmed and cut into ½-inch cubes

1 red bell pepper, cored, seeded, deveined, and cut into ¼-inch cubes

1 cup raw converted rice

2 sprigs fresh thyme, or ½ teaspoon dried

1 bay leaf

2 tablespoons chopped fresh coriander (cilantro)

Dash of Tabasco sauce

Salt and freshly ground pepper, to taste

1. Over medium-high heat, heat the olive oil in a large, heavy saucepan with a tight-fitting lid. Add the onion, garlic, zucchini, and red pepper. Stir until wilted.

2. Add the rice and stir to blend. Cook briefly, then add the thyme, bay leaf, coriander, Tabasco, salt, and pepper. Add 1½ cups water and bring to a boil, stirring, then cover tightly. Reduce the heat to medium and simmer for 17 minutes.

3. Uncover and remove the thyme sprig and bay leaf. Stir with a fork to fluff rice lightly before serving.

APPLE AÏOLI

YIELD: ABOUT 1¼ CUPS

Although some cooks like to spread this sauce over food, I prefer to serve it as a garnish. The Aïoli can be kept for several days if refrigerated. It is delicious with seafood, meat, or poultry.

1 Golden Delicious apple

1 tablespoon Dijon mustard

2 tablespoons chopped garlic

Salt and freshly ground white pepper, to taste

Dash of Tabasco sauce

½ cup olive oil

1. Peel and core the apple. Cut it into thin slices, then place in a saucepan with ¼ cup water. Cover and bring to a boil, then cook for 2 minutes. Let cool.

2. In a blender or food processor, combine the cooled apple and juices, mustard, garlic, salt, white pepper, and Tabasco. While processing, add the olive oil quickly—within about 30 seconds—until the aïoli is of fine texture. Check for seasoning and serve cool.

SEAFOOD SALAD

YIELD: 4-6 SERVINGS

This is one of my favorite dishes for the summer. It is important that you watch the cooking time—do not over-cook the seafood, because it will dry out, shrink in size, and become rubbery.

2 pounds mussels, well scrubbed and beards removed
½ teaspoon dried thyme
1 bay leaf
2 tablespoons white wine vinegar
1 pint sea or bay scallops
½ pound raw medium shrimp, peeled and deveined
Salt and freshly ground pepper, to taste
½ pound snow peas, trimmed and strings removed
1 ripe unblemished mango (about ½ pound)
1 small head Chinese (napa) cabbage
1 bunch red leaf lettuce
½ cup chopped scallions
Ginger Vinaigrette (see following page)
⅓ cup finely chopped herbs, such as parsley, chives, and tarragon

1. Place the mussels in a large pot and add the thyme, bay leaf, and vinegar. Cover, bring to a boil over high heat, and cook 3 minutes or until the mussels are opened. Remove from the heat.

2. Drain the mussels, reserving the cooking liquid. Discard any mussels that have not opened. Strain the liquid through a fine sieve or cheesecloth. There should be ½ cup.

3. Pour the mussel liquid into a clean saucepan and add the scallops. Cover and bring to a boil. Reduce heat and simmer about 1 minute. Add the shrimp, salt, and pepper. Cook about 1 minute. Remove from the heat and drain. Let cool.

4. Meanwhile, remove the mussels from their shells.

5. Place the snow peas in a saucepan; add cold water to cover and salt. Bring to a boil over high heat and simmer about 2 minutes. Drain.

6. Peel the mango, then carefully cut away the flesh from the pit. Cut the flesh into slices or ½-inch cubes.

7. Cut the cabbage and lettuce into thin shreds.

8. In a bowl, combine the cabbage, lettuce, mango, snow peas, and scallions. Add ¼ cup of the vinaigrette and toss to blend.

9. Divide the tossed mixture among 4 large serving plates, piling up neatly. Arrange the mussels, scallops, and shrimp neatly over all. Pour more vinaigrette over, sprinkle with herbs, and serve.

GINGER VINAIGRETTE

YIELD: ¾ CUP

This vinaigrette goes well with any seafood but especially well with broiled fish. It also is tasty with broiled meat and can be used in many different kinds of salads.

1 tablespoon Dijon mustard
1 tablespoon grated fresh ginger
2 tablespoons finely chopped shallots
1 teaspoon finely chopped garlic
2 tablespoons red wine vinegar
¼ cup finely chopped red bell pepper
2 tablespoons chopped fresh coriander (cilantro)
Dash of Tabasco sauce
Salt and freshly ground pepper, to taste
¼ cup olive or corn oil

1. Place the mustard, ginger, shallots, garlic, vinegar, red pepper, coriander, Tabasco, salt, and pepper in a small mixing bowl. Blend well with a wire whisk.

2. Add the oil slowly, whisking rapidly until well blended. Check for seasoning.

*A lively meeting of the all-male
San Sebastián Gastronomic Society.*

POACHED PEARS IN PORT WINE

—

YIELD: 8 SERVINGS

Although there are many kinds of pears on the market, my favorites are Bartlett and Bosc because of their sweetness and size. Any ripe, unblemished pear will do, however. You can use any wine, red or white, in this recipe as well. If using a sweet wine, reduce the amount of sugar.

8 ripe Bartlett or Bosc pears (about 2 pounds total)
Juice of 1 lemon
1¼ cups Port wine
¼ cup honey
½ cup sugar
4 black peppercorns
2 whole cloves
1 small bay leaf
2 sprigs fresh thyme, or ¼ teaspoon dried

1. Peel the pears with a vegetable peeler and remove the core with a corer. The pears can be left whole or halved or quartered.

2. Place the pears in a saucepan large enough to hold them standing upright. Add all the remaining ingredients, blend well, bring just to a boil, cover, and simmer over very low heat for about 30 minutes.

3. Remove the pears from the pan and stand them upright in a serving bowl. Strain the sauce over the pears and allow them to cool before serving. Baste the pears periodically with the wine sauce as they cool. Cover and refrigerate.

BAY SCALLOPS IN SHALLOT SAUCE

YIELD: 4 SERVINGS

If bay scallops are not available, use sea scallops and cut them into halves or quarters according to size. But caution: this dish has to be cooked very quickly over high heat so the scallops do not overcook and become tough.

1 quart bay scallops

Salt and freshly ground pepper, to taste

4 tablespoons olive oil

1 large red bell pepper, cored, seeded, and cut into ¼-inch cubes

6 tablespoons chopped shallots

¼ cup fine fresh bread crumbs

2 tablespoons lemon juice

1 teaspoon Worcestershire sauce

2 tablespoons chopped chives or parsley

1. Sprinkle the scallops with salt and pepper.

2. Heat 2 tablespoons olive oil in a heavy nonstick skillet large enough to hold the scallops in one layer. Add the scallops and cook over high heat, shaking the skillet and stirring them so they cook evenly, for about 2 minutes. Add the red pepper and cook, stirring, for 2 minutes over high heat. Add the shallots, remaining 2 tablespoons olive oil, and bread crumbs. Cook over high heat 2 minutes more, then add the lemon juice and Worcestershire sauce. Cook about 30 seconds, blending and mixing. Add the chives or parsley, stir, and serve.

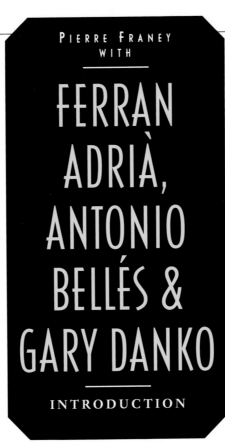

FERRAN ADRIÀ, ANTONIO BELLÉS & GARY DANKO

INTRODUCTION

With great anticipation, I traveled north from Barcelona up the Costa Brava to visit Ferran Adrià, a young Spanish chef whose innovative cuisine has brought him international fame. But getting to his restaurant, El Bulli, was no easy task. It is located in Cala Montjoy, a small fishing village in the Catalan region, and the last half-hour of the drive is over a twisting dirt road that winds up and down the high coastal hills. Beautiful views of the rugged Mediterranean coastline were accompanied by fields of wild pink roses and bright yellow flowers called *genista*. Avoiding potholes, we drove down into the small cove and came upon the most spectacular setting for a restaurant. Perched on a rocky hill above the bay and surrounded by flowers and herb gardens, El Bulli offers marvelous views in every direction.

The entrance to El Bulli, situated on the rugged Costa Brava coast.

Ferran's cuisine is inspired by the world around him. His motto, "inspiration, adaptation and association," describes his style of cooking. Nature plays a big role—for example, after observing an azalea bush in full bloom, he returned to his kitchen and created a salad of red beets cut into the shape of fine, delicate petals. Señor Adrià has no formal culinary training; he taught himself to cook by observing master chefs such as Paul Bocuse and Michel Guérard, studying Escoffier's tome on classic French cooking, and eating in many different restaurants throughout Europe. He believes in the evolution of food and the modernization of classical cooking. His menu includes a lot of very fresh local seafood, vegetables, fruits, and light sauces that have been greatly reduced to bring an intensity of flavor to the palate. He avoids heavy sauces with a lot of fat and uses a variety of local Spanish olive oils flavored, for example, with vanilla or chile pepper.

The kitchen at El Bulli is a pleasure to work in. It has large floor-to-ceiling glass windows that look out onto the gardens around the restaurant. In the middle of one worktable sits the carved wooden head of a large bull. Ferran leads a kitchen staff of young men and women who spend hours cutting, cleaning, and meticulously preparing the food to be cooked. His partner, Julio Soler, is responsible for the management of the dining room.

During my visit to El Bulli, Ferran prepared a variety of low-fat dishes for me. One of my favorites was mangoes sliced very thin, then cut to look like noodles and placed overlapping on a plate, sprinkled with two olive oils and chopped fresh basil. This was one of his "trick" dishes, where eyes tell you one thing (noodles) but the taste is a surprise (mangoes). It can be served as an appetizer; as an accompaniment to langoustine, lobster, or foie gras; or as a dessert served with fruit (eliminating the oils). He also prepared one of his most popular dishes, Langoustine Wrapped with Cèpes (see page 57), which he has been serving in his restaurant for eight years. One of the tricks in preparing this dish is to freeze the mushrooms in advance, which makes it easier to cut them into very thin slices with a sharp knife. This is one example of Ferran's innovative cooking while maintaining a low-fat approach to food.

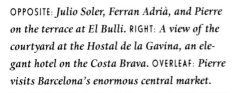

OPPOSITE: *Julio Soler, Ferran Adrià, and Pierre on the terrace at El Bulli.* RIGHT: *A view of the courtyard at the Hostal de la Gavina, an elegant hotel on the Costa Brava.* OVERLEAF: *Pierre visits Barcelona's enormous central market.*

FROM FERRAN ADRIÀ

LANGOUSTINE WRAPPED WITH CÈPES

❧

QUAIL LEG APPETIZERS

FROM ANTONIO BELLÉS

MARINATED SEAFOOD SALAD

❧

PAN CON TOMATE

FROM GARY DANKO

LIGHT ORANGE SOUFFLÉ

❧

WARM CHOCOLATE SAUCE

FROM PIERRE FRANEY

GRILLED TUNA WITH CAPERS AND TOMATO SAUCE

❧

BROILED FRESH ASPARAGUS

❧

GAZPACHO

❧

ESCABÈCHE OF MIXED VEGETABLES

❧

SHRIMP ON SKEWERS
WITH LIGHT TARTAR SAUCE

❧

BAKED COD WITH POTATOES

❧

SAUTÉED SPANISH CHICKEN

LANGOUSTINE WRAPPED WITH CÈPES

YIELD: 4 SERVINGS

Ferran Adrià used live langoustine for this recipe. However, fresh langoustine are not easily available in the United States. They have to be flown in from Europe or South America, and hence are very expensive. The meat is very tender and sweet. A good substitute is large Hawaiian shrimp or jumbo shrimp (4-6 to a pound).

4 large fresh langoustine or very large shrimp (3 ounces each)

2 large fresh mushrooms, such as cèpes or boletus, about 2 ½ inches in diameter

2 tablespoons sunflower oil

16 fresh young scallions

1½ teaspoons coarsley chopped toasted pine nuts

¼ cup olive oil

1 tablespoon sherry vinegar

2 tablespoons chopped chives

l hard goat cheese (about 2 ounces), cut into 20 ¼-inch cubes

Salt, to taste

1.   Separate the tail from the body of each langoustine. Remove the shell from around the tail, leaving the tail fan attached. Remove the central intestine by twisting the center section of the fan of the tail and pulling gently, removing the intestine at the same time. If using shrimp, remove the head, shell, and intestine running along the back.

2.   Clean the mushrooms with a damp cloth. Cut each stem from its cap with a knife. Place the caps in the freezer for 4–5 hours, or until partially frozen. Remove and cut with a very sharp knife into thin even slices, ⅛ inch thick or less.

3.   Over medium heat, put 1 tablespoon sunflower oil in a medium nonstick sauté pan. Add the mushroom slices and cook briefly, only until wilted and flexible. Lay the slices out on a towel to drain.

4.   Arrange 8 mushroom slices on a plate horizontally, starting with the largest and overlapping each slightly. Place 1 langoustine in the center and roll the edges over each side to wrap the tail entirely with a solid layer of mushrooms. Repeat for remaining langoustine.

5.   Place the scallions in a sauté pan and cover with cold water. Bring to a boil and cook over high heat for 30 seconds. Remove, drain, and cool. Peel off the first outer layer and trim the root.

6.   Combine the remaining ingredients in a small bowl and toss to mix.

7.   Place the remaining sunflower oil in a medium nonstick sauté pan over very high heat. Add the blanched scallions and sauté, about 1 minute. Remove to a plate. Add the langoustine and cook on both sides until the mushrooms are browned and the langoustine are cooked, about 1 minute on each side.

8.   To serve, lay 4 scallions over each plate. Place a langoustine or shrimp on top and spoon the vinaigrette around.

QUAIL LEG APPETIZERS

—

YIELD: 4 SERVINGS

Ferran calls these his "quail lollipops" because the meat is pushed down the drumstick and sits on one end of the bone. It is one of the playful tricks in his personal cuisine. Although he uses only the legs, you can also cook the breast meat this way, with the bone removed.

8 fresh quail
Sunflower oil, for frying
½ cup all-purpose flour, for dusting
¼ cup soy sauce

1. With a sharp knife, remove the legs from the quail. Separate the thigh from the drumstick. Push the meat down the thigh bones with your fingers or a knife and remove the thigh bone.

2. Hold the drumstick with the meat attached and cut the tendon at the ankle of the drumstick. Pull the meat down the bone to form a pear shape, with the clean leg bone extended.

3. In a medium nonstick skillet, heat ½ inch of oil to 340° F.

4. Dust the drumsticks lightly with flour, making sure they are coated well. Remove any excess flour.

5. Carefully drop all the drumsticks into the hot oil and fry until lightly brown and cooked, about 15 minutes. Remove and drain on paper towels.

6. To serve, place the soy sauce in a small bowl, and serve as dipping sauce.

*T*apas bars are found throughout Spain. They are a popular place to go before lunch or dinner, although some people enjoy having a full meal there. The bar is covered from one end to the other with small, tantalizing dishes ranging from a plate of olives to an assortment of creative dishes made with cheese, sausage, seafood, vegetables, and ham—all prepared in different ways. The tapas are best eaten while sipping a glass of sherry or a local sparkling wine.

In the tapas bar of the Hotel Arts, chef Antonio Bellés drizzles a finishing touch of Spanish olive oil on Pan con Tomate as Pierre and friend Emmanuel Kemiji look on.

Tapas are believed to have originated centuries ago, when horsemen traveled from town to town, arriving hungry and thirsty. Tavern-keepers prepared glasses of wine covered by a tapa, or lid, made of a slice of ham, sausage, or country bread. This lid protected the wine from dust, rain, and flies. Over the years, each region of Spain developed its own tapas specialties, and today's chefs are also quite innovative in their creations.

One talented chef is Antonio Bellés, the 1995 Chef of the Year in Spain. I visited with him at the Goyescas Room, the tapas bar at the Hotel Arts in Barcelona. Antonio prepared an amazing array of tapas that included fresh anchovies marinated in oil, brochetta of monkfish wrapped in pancetta, snails braised in wine, fried calamari, roasted calf's liver, and shrimp with roasted peppers. He also prepared a delicious Marinated Seafood Salad that is low in fat simply because it is made with only 1 tablespoon of oil. The salad should be served with a classic Spanish bread—Pan con Tomate (see page 60).

MARINATED SEAFOOD SALAD

YIELD: 4 SERVINGS

Using fresh seafood and vegetables is the key to making this delicious salad. Serve with Pan con Tomate (see below).

4 baby octopus
4 large raw shrimp, shelled and deveined
8 bay scallops
1 large, very ripe tomato, cored and cubed
¼ cup cored, seeded, and diced red bell pepper
¼ cup cored, seeded, and diced green bell pepper
¼ cup thinly sliced onion
4 sprigs watercress, large stems removed
2 tablespoons black olives
1 tablespoon olive oil
1 teaspoon sherry vinegar
Salt and freshly ground pepper, to taste

1. Bring water to a boil in the bottom of a steamer. Add the octopus and steam for 15 minutes. Then add the shrimp and scallops and steam for 3 minutes more. Remove and let cool.

2. In a large salad bowl, combine the seafood and tomato, bell pepper, onion, watercress, and olives.

3. Add the oil and vinegar, then salt and pepper. Toss well and serve.

PAN CON TOMATE

YIELD: 4 SERVINGS

In Spain, country bread is crusty and coarsely textured. Antonio Bellés serves this with tapas at the Goyescas Room of the Hotel Arts in Barcelona.

4 slices country bread, ½ inch thick
1 garlic clove, split in half
2 large, very ripe tomatoes, cut in half crosswise
3 tablespoons olive oil, preferably Catalan
Salt, to taste

1. Toast the bread slices and rub each slice with half a garlic clove. Rub a tomato half on each slice, making sure some flesh and juice are left on the bread, leaving only the skin of the tomato in your hand. Drizzle with olive oil and season with salt before serving.

While in Barcelona I visited Gary Danko, an accomplished American chef who has created a California-style menu at the Newport Room of the Hotel Arts in Barcelona. Gary is the dining room chef of the highly acclaimed restaurant at the Ritz-Carlton in San Francisco, and he also spends part of his time designing new menus for restaurants around the world. At the beautiful and modern Newport Room in Barcelona, the combination of California cuisine and local Spanish products was a perfect fit. The end result is a menu that is not only light and nutritious but also uses the best and freshest Spanish ingredients. Here is a sample of one of Gary's low-fat desserts, Light Orange Soufflé (see page 62), which uses a marmalade of Spanish oranges.

LIGHT ORANGE SOUFFLÉ

YIELD: 4 SERVINGS

This is a low-fat soufflé because it uses no egg yolks in the base. The chocolate sauce, however, does add some fat.

Any chef will tell you that egg whites are best whipped by hand in a copper bowl to get that light and airy quality as well as greater volume. Here's an easy way to clean a copper bowl: Make a paste of 4 tablespoons flour, 2 tablespoons salt, and 2-3 tablespoons white vinegar. Rub the mixture with a sponge over the inside and outside of the bowl—or even better, use half a lemon to rub the mixture over the bowl. Rinse with cold water.

¼ cup granulated sugar
½ cup good-quality chunky orange marmalade
1 tablespoon Grand Marnier
4 large egg whites
Confectioners' sugar
Warm Chocolate Sauce (see following page)

1.   Preheat the oven to 400° F.

2.   Spray four 1-cup soufflé molds with vegetable cooking spray, or brush with 1 tablespoon melted butter. Dust with granulated sugar, removing excess sugar, and set aside in a cool place.

3.   Place marmalade in a large mixing bowl. Using a wire whisk, combine well with the Grand Marnier.

4.   Beat the egg whites in a large, very clean copper bowl with a balloon whisk until they form soft peaks.

5.   Fold the whites into the marmalade mixture, blending well. Spoon into the prepared molds and level with a spatula. Make a channel around the edge of the molds using a thumb.

6.   Bake for 8-10 minutes. Sprinkle with confectioners' sugar and serve immediately with the chocolate sauce. To serve, make a hole in the center of the soufflé and pour in as much sauce as desired.

WARM CHOCOLATE SAUCE

YIELD: 1½ CUPS

The quality of this chocolate sauce will depend on the type of chocolate you use. Be sure to use an excellent one.

2 tablespoons unsweetened cocoa powder
2 tablespoons sugar
4 ounces semisweet chocolate, broken into pieces
1 tablespoon Grand Marnier

1. In a medium saucepan over medium heat, combine the cocoa powder, ¾ cup water, and the sugar. Bring to a boil.

2. Remove from the heat and add the chocolate and Grand Marnier. Stir until melted. Serve warm.

Chef Gary Danko pours Warm Chocolate Sauce into the center of his Light Orange Soufflé.

GRILLED TUNA WITH CAPERS AND TOMATO SAUCE

YIELD: 4 SERVINGS

I always enjoy going to fish markets and deciding what to cook that day. This way I can pick what fish looks most fresh to me. The fish market in Barcelona was wonderful, with an amazing array of seafood. The tuna I bought was very fresh, and I cooked it with a light sauce of capers and tomatoes. The tomatoes, purchased in the same market, caught my eye because they were so red and fresh-looking.

4 center cut tuna steaks (about 4-5 ounces each)
2 tablespoons olive oil
Salt and freshly ground pepper, to taste
¼ teaspoon hot red pepper flakes
4 sprigs fresh thyme, coarsely chopped, or 1 teaspoon dried
⅓ cup drained capers
4 small, ripe plum tomatoes, cored and cut into small cubes
1 tablespoon fresh lemon juice
4 tablespoons chopped fresh basil or parsley

1. Prepare a charcoal grill or preheat the broiler.

2. Place the tuna on a flat dish and spoon 1 tablespoon oil over it. Sprinkle with salt and pepper, red pepper flakes, and thyme, and spread well into the steaks. Cover with plastic wrap and let stand at least 15 minutes before grilling.

3. Heat the remaining tablespoon olive oil in a small skillet. Add the capers and cook briefly over medium-high heat. Add the tomatoes, salt and pepper, and lemon juice, and cook for about 5 minutes. Keep warm.

4. If using a grill, rub the rack lightly with olive oil. Place the fish on the grill and cook for 3 minutes, then turn and cook for another 3 minutes for rare. If you wish the fish to be more well done, cook longer on each side. If broiling, place in pan and broil for 6 minutes for rare, turning once.

5. Remove the fish and cut it into thin diagonal slices. To serve, divide the tomatoes among 4 warm plates. Place the tuna slices on top and sprinkle with basil or parsley.

BROILED FRESH ASPARAGUS

YIELD: 4 SERVINGS

I think it is important to peel asparagus because the outside layer is always tough. By removing this layer, you guarantee a more tender texture and a more pleasing flavor. Be sure not to overcook— asparagus should be served tender-crisp.

24 medium asparagus
2 tablespoons olive oil
¼ teaspoon grated nutmeg
Salt and freshly ground pepper, to taste

1. Preheat the broiler.

2. Snap off the tough stems of each asparagus. Peel using a swivel-bladed paring knife, leaving 2 inches of the tips intact.

3. Bring salted water to a boil in a saucepan large enough to fit the asparagus. When the water boils, add the asparagus and simmer for 1-2 minutes, depending on the size. The asparagus should be firm but tender. Drain immediately.

4. Blend the olive oil, nutmeg, salt, and pepper and brush over the drained asparagus.

5. Place the asparagus on a broiler pan and broil for about 2 minutes, turning them occasionally. They should be lightly browned. Do not overcook.

GAZPACHO

—

YIELD: 4-6 SERVINGS

Gazpacho is a classic Spanish soup that should be served well chilled. The success of any gazpacho is in the freshness of the ingredients. Be sure the tomatoes are ripe and juicy. I prefer a gazpacho that has a crunchy texture. If you prefer a smoother soup, blend the mixture longer.

3 small cucumbers (about 1 pound)
8 ripe plum tomatoes (about 1½ pounds)
1½ cups coarsely chopped red onion
1 tablespoon finely chopped garlic
1½ cups finely diced red bell pepper
2 tablespoons red wine vinegar
2 tablespoons fresh lemon juice
2 tablespoons olive oil
½ cup tomato juice
¼ teaspoon Tabasco sauce
Salt and freshly ground white pepper, to taste

FOR GARNISH

½ cup finely chopped cucumber
1 cup finely chopped green bell pepper
½ cup finely chopped peeled and seeded ripe tomatoes
1 cup toasted bread cubes
4 tablespoons coarsely chopped fresh coriander (cilantro)

1. Peel the cucumbers and cut them lengthwise in half. Remove the seeds and cut them into small cubes, yielding about 2 cups.

2. Drop the tomatoes into boiling water for 10 seconds. Remove and let cool. Peel and core, then dice the tomatoes. Reserve the seeds and juice. There should be about 3 cups of tomatoes.

3. Place the cucumbers, tomatoes, reserved tomato juice and seeds, and red onion in a food processor or blender. Add the garlic, red bell pepper, vinegar, lemon juice, olive oil, tomato juice, Tabasco, salt, and pepper. Blend quickly—the texture should be coarse. Place the mixture in a nonreactive bowl and refrigerate until thoroughly chilled. Check for seasoning.

4. Serve the soup, preferably in chilled bowls, with the garnish in separate bowls on the side.

BAKED COD WITH POTATOES

—

YIELD: 4-6 SERVINGS

This recipe can also be made with center-cut cod steaks with the bone in. The cooking time is the same. Test for doneness by making sure the bone pulls away from the fish easily.

4 tablespoons olive oil

Salt and freshly ground pepper, to taste

4 boneless center-cut cod steaks (5-6 ounces each), about 2 inches thick, skin removed

1½ pounds potatoes

¾ cup thinly sliced small white onions

½ cup dry white wine

1 teaspoon finely chopped garlic

2 tablespoons chopped parsley

3 tablespoons fresh bread crumbs

1.　Preheat the oven to 425° F.

2.　Brush a flameproof baking dish with 2 tablespoons olive oil. It must be large enough to hold the steaks in one layer with the potatoes. Sprinkle the bottom of the dish with salt and pepper. Arrange the cod in one layer on the bottom.

3.　Peel and slice the potatoes thinly. Place them in a saucepan with water to cover, bring to a boil, and drain immediately in a colander.

4.　Scatter the potato slices and the onions around the cod but not on top. Salt and pepper to taste. Add the wine and ½ cup water.

5.　Combine the garlic, parsley, and bread crumbs and blend well. Sprinkle over the fish.

6.　Place the baking dish on top of the stove and bring to a boil, then reduce the heat and simmer for 5 minutes.

7.　Put the baking dish in the oven and bake for 20 minutes or until the potatoes and onions are cooked and the top is slightly browned. Test the fish for doneness by piercing the center of the cod steak with the tip of a paring knife. The fish should be white and flaky.

SAUTÉED SPANISH CHICKEN

YIELD: 4 SERVINGS

Spanish onions are nice and sweet. This recipe calls for saffron, which is commonly used in Spanish cooking. It is important to use only saffron that comes in threads, not powdered. The threads have much more flavor. If you don't like the taste of saffron, substitute turmeric, which has a mild taste and is used mostly for coloring.

1 3- to 3½-pound chicken, cut into 10 serving pieces,
    with excess skin and fat removed

Salt and freshly ground pepper, to taste

1 tablespoon olive oil

½ cup finely chopped Spanish onion

1 tablespoon finely chopped garlic

2 cups coarsely chopped red and green bell peppers

1 teaspoon loosely packed saffron threads,
    or 1 teaspoon turmeric

½ cup dry white wine

2 cups peeled and diced plum tomatoes

1 bay leaf

2 sprigs fresh thyme, or ½ teaspoon dried

Hot red pepper flakes, to taste

2 tablespoons finely chopped basil or parsley, for garnish

1. Sprinkle the chicken pieces with salt and pepper. Set aside.

2. Heat the olive oil in a heavy skillet large enough to hold the pieces in one layer. Add the chicken skin side down and cook over medium-high heat for 5 minutes or until nicely browned on one side. Turn and continue cooking, turning occasionally, for about 5 minutes more.

3. Remove the chicken and drain off most of the fat, then add the onion, garlic, peppers, and saffron. Cook over medium heat, stirring, for about 1 minute. Add the wine and stir the bottom of the skillet to dissolve the brown particles. Add the tomatoes, bay leaf, thyme, red pepper flakes, and the chicken. Cover and cook for 20 minutes. Uncover and cook 10 minutes longer if necessary. The chicken is done when the meat comes away from the thigh bone easily and any juices run clear. Check for seasoning.

4. If you want to reduce the fat content, remove the skin from the chicken. Serve sprinkled with basil or parsley.

PIERRE FRANEY
WITH

BRUNA & NADIA SANTINI

INTRODUCTION

When I planned my visit to Italy, the one restaurant I did not want to miss was Dal Pescatore. Located in the quiet Italian countryside about an hour from the city of Parma, it is one of the top restaurants in Italy. Truly a country restaurant, it is owned by the Santini family, who are involved in the day-to-day running of this third-generation, very successful enterprise. Dal Pescatore rates three stars (the highest rating) in the prestigious *Guide Michelin* to hotels and restaurants.

I first met Bruna Santini when she came to New York and spent a week cooking at Le Cirque, the restaurant of my friend Sirio Maccioni. Sirio invited me to watch her

cook, and I was impressed with her respect for traditional Italian cuisine, her uncomplicated style of cooking, and her insistence on the freshest ingredients. And that is exactly what I found at her family restaurant in the small town of Cannetto sul Oglio.

RIGHT: *A quiet corner in the dining room at Dal Pescatore.*
OPPOSITE: *A decanted glass of 1982 Barolo awaits.*

— *73* —

ABOVE: *An exuberant Pierre with Bruna and Nadia Santini in the Dal Pescatore kitchen.* OPPOSITE: *A window-side table in one of the private dining rooms.* OVERLEAF: *The front entrance to the ivy-covered restaurant.*

Dal Pescatore is a warm and inviting restaurant—one that makes you feel as if you were in a private home. The marble floors are covered with flowered rugs, antiques are everywhere, and family photographs adorn the walls. The restaurant was started in 1920 by Grandfather Santini, who bought a house and converted it into a trattoria, serving fresh fish that he caught daily and the favorite local wine, Lambrusco. His wife did all the cooking. Today, Bruna and her daughter-in-law, Nadia Santini, are the chefs, the two women working side by side. Antonio, Nadia's charming husband, runs the dining room. And her father-in-law, Giovanni Santini, oversees the farm and garden behind the restaurant.

One of the keys to the success of this restaurant is the insistence on using fresh local produce. Giovanni raises his own chickens, ducks, and rabbits. Because the chickens are fed leftovers from the restaurant, the eggs are of rich quality. This enables Bruna to have the very best eggs to make her pasta, for which the restaurant is famous. Fish are caught in traps set in the river that runs in the back. They are kept alive in a fish pond and are scooped out with a big net just before they are cooked. The day I was there, the pond was filled with eels and pike. And the garden has an enormous variety of vegetables. It was there that I picked my own baby spinach, peas, and basil for a pasta dish I created on the spot (Penne with Baby Spinach and Fresh Peas, page 84).

Nadia's cooking, though based on traditional Italian cuisine, is not high in fat. She believes that food should be cooked simply, and not drowned in sauces. For instance, she uses just enough sauce to bind the pasta. Grated cheese is served on the side to allow diners to decide on the amount. Fish and vegetables are an important part of the menu. Her mother-in-law's pasta is rich and made with many eggs, but one need not have a large serving to feel sated. The two recipes Nadia demonstrated for us were quickly cooked in a bit of olive oil. The flavor came from the fresh fish and the right combination of accompanying vegetables. They are a perfect example of the Santini's philosophy of cooking: a respect for tradition, simplicity, and fresh ingredients.

PIKE WITH PARSLEY SAUCE

YIELD: 4 SERVINGS

Dal Pescatore has a pond on the premises so the fish is incredibly fresh. Nadia's father-in-law goes out to the pond with a big net and scoops out the fish for the evening's meal. Serve this pike with polenta (see page 87).

2 6-ounce fillets of large freshwater fish, such as northern
    pike or trout, scaled, with bones and skin left on
½ lemon
2 tablespoons olive oil
2 anchovy fillets
1½ garlic cloves
2 tablespoons capers in salt, rinsed
4 tablespoons chopped parsley

1. Place the fish in a small saucepan with the lemon half and add enough water to cover. Bring to a boil, simmer 2 minutes, and turn off the heat. Let fish rest in the water until it has cooled.

2. When cool, debone the fish. Remove from the water, cut each piece in half and remove the bones with a pair of tweezers or small pair of pliers. Remove the skin by scraping with a sharp knife.

3. Heat the olive oil in an 8-inch nonstick skillet. Add the anchovies, garlic, and capers, and cook briefly, just to warm. Add the parsley, remove pan from heat and set aside.

4. Place the fish in the center of a plate and spoon the sauce around.

PASTA WITH SAVOY CABBAGE

YIELD: 4 SERVINGS

Savoy cabbage is curly-leafed and not packed as tightly as regular green cabbage. I find that the leaves are very tender and it cooks quickly. Nadia used her mother-in-law's homemade tagliatelle. Bruna is well known in Parma for her fresh pasta; people come from all over the world to eat it.

1 medium savoy cabbage

8 ounces fresh (see following page) or store-bought tagliatelle or fettuccine

4 tablespoons extra-virgin olive oil

2 tablespoons coarsely sliced scallions

Salt and freshly ground pepper, to taste

3 anchovy fillets, coarsely chopped

1. Remove and discard the outer leaves of the cabbage. With a knife, remove the core and shred the tender leaves. You should have about 2 cups of packed, shredded leaves.

2. Bring a large pot of salted water to a boil. Add the pasta and stir gently to prevent sticking. Cook according to the directions on the package, stirring occasionally and taking care not to overcook.

3. In the meantime, place 2 tablespoons of olive oil in a large nonstick skillet. Add the scallions and cook until wilted. Add the cabbage and season with salt and pepper. Sauté quickly until wilted and tender but still crunchy, stirring often.

4. In a separate nonstick skillet, heat the remaining 2 tablespoons olive oil. Add the anchovy fillets and sauté briefly, a minute or two.

5. Drain the pasta and add to the anchovy and olive oil mixture. Toss well to combine. Add the cabbage and scallion mixture and toss well. Serve immediately.

NOTE: Nadia Santini suggests that this pasta dish be served with a mixed green salad and grated Parmesan cheese on the side.

PASTA DOUGH

**YIELD: PASTA FOR
10-12 SERVINGS**

*At Dal Pescatore,
Bruna includes one
duck egg yolk in her
pasta recipe because
it gives the dough
higher elasticity and
a richer color. If you
do not have a duck
egg, just use an
extra chicken egg.
Obviously, this is
not a low-fat pasta,
but I wanted to
include it because I
was so impressed
with its texture and
high quality. Fresh
pasta cooks
quickly—one or two
minutes only.*

4 cups all-purpose flour
7 large egg yolks plus 1 duck egg yolk
1 large whole egg
Salt, to taste

1. Pour the flour onto a wooden table and make a well in the center using your fist. Place the egg yolks and whole egg in the center of the flour with the salt.

2. Begin to mix the eggs using a small spatula, gradually incorporating more and more flour from the edges to achieve a smooth paste. Divide the dough into 4 rectangular pieces 1 inch thick.

3. Roll out the dough by hand if you are expert in pasta making or, if using a pasta machine, roll out according to the manufacturer's instructions.

4. Cut the pasta into desired shapes, such as squares for ravioli or tortellini, or cut into spaghetti, fettuccine, tagliatelle, or angelhair pasta. Wrap in plastic wrap and refrigerate for up to 24 hours if you want to make the pasta in advance.

*Bruna Santini makes
her extraordinary
pasta in the Dal
Pescatore kitchen.*

AVOCADO AND MUSHROOM SALAD

YIELD: 4 SERVINGS

Although avocados are high in fat, they are low in sodium and contain no cholesterol. Here I have used only one avocado to serve four people and have added mushrooms and red bell pepper, which have no fat.

1 small red bell pepper
1 tablespoon Dijon mustard
1 tablespoon red wine vinegar
1 tablespoon finely chopped shallots
Salt and freshly ground pepper, to taste
3 tablespoons olive oil
¼ pound fresh mushrooms, thinly sliced
1 firm, ripe medium avocado
2 tablespoons finely chopped parsley

1. Cut away the core and veins of the pepper and discard the seeds. Cut the pepper into thin slices.

2. Combine the mustard, vinegar, shallots, salt, and pepper in a large salad bowl; blend well with a wire whisk. Gradually add the olive oil until well blended. Add the mushrooms and red pepper.

3. Peel the avocado and cut in half. Remove and discard the pit. Cut flesh into 1-inch cubes. Add the avocado and parsley to the salad, toss gently, and blend well.

SAUTÉED ESCAROLE

YIELD: 4 SERVINGS

This green is very popular in Italy. Here I sauté it lightly with garlic and a bit of lemon.

1½ pounds escarole
1 tablespoon olive oil
1 teaspoon finely minced garlic
2 teaspoons fresh lemon juice
Salt and freshly ground pepper, to taste

1. Cut out the core of the escarole, trim the ends, and remove any blemished outside leaves. Rinse well.

2. Drop the escarole into boiling salted water. Simmer until tender, about 5 minutes. Drain well and squeeze to extract excess liquid.

3. Heat the olive oil in a large nonstick skillet and add the garlic, lemon juice, and escarole, stirring and taking care not to brown the garlic. Add salt and pepper and cook, stirring, until warm.

MEDALLIONS OF LAMB WITH BASIL

YIELD: 4 SERVINGS

Lamb has a lower fat content than beef and the outer fat can be easily removed. When cooking these medallions, it is very important to sear the meat quickly on all sides. They can be served with sautéed potatoes or any kind of vegetable.

2 boned loins or racks of lamb (about 1½ pounds), all fat removed
4 ripe plum tomatoes (about 1 pound)
2 tablespoons olive oil
2 teaspoons finely chopped garlic
¼ cup chopped fresh basil
Salt and freshly ground pepper, to taste
1 teaspoon ground cumin
2 sprigs fresh thyme, or ½ teaspoon dried
2 tablespoons finely chopped shallots
3 tablespoons coarsely chopped basil or parsley

1. Cut the lamb into 12 pieces of equal size. Pound them lightly with a meat pounder or mallet.

2. Drop the tomatoes into a pot of boiling water for 10 seconds. Remove and let cool. When the tomatoes have cooled, remove the skins, core them, and cut into ¼-inch chunks. There should be about 1½ cups.

3. Heat 1 tablespoon olive oil in a large saucepan over medium-high heat. Add the garlic and cook briefly until soft but not brown. Add the tomatoes, basil, salt, and pepper. Stir, lower heat, and simmer for 5 minutes. Keep warm.

4. Blend salt and pepper to taste with the cumin and sprinkle over the lamb medallions.

5. Heat 1 tablespoon of olive oil in a nonstick skillet large enough to hold the pieces in one layer. Add the lamb and the thyme. Brown the lamb quickly on all sides and cook over relatively high heat, about 2 minutes on each side for rare or longer if desired. Remove the lamb to a warm platter.

6. In the same pan, add the shallots and cook briefly, stirring until wilted. Add the tomato mixture and any meat juices that have accumulated in the platter and blend well.

7. To serve, divide the tomato sauce evenly among 4 plates. Place 3 pieces of lamb over the sauce on each plate and garnish with chopped basil or parsley.

PENNE WITH BABY SPINACH AND FRESH PEAS

YIELD: 4 SERVINGS

I created this recipe while walking through the vegetable garden at Dal Pescatore. I was impressed with the variety of vegetables grown behind the restaurant, and I picked the baby spinach, fresh peas, and basil myself. Although I am not a big fan of vegetarian cooking, this is a delicious pasta and vegetable dish that is good for a light lunch or dinner. The Parmesan cheese is optional and can be served on the side.

8 ounces penne pasta
½ cup shelled fresh peas
2 tablespoons olive oil
1 tablespoon finely chopped garlic
¼ teaspoon hot red pepper flakes, or to taste
4 ripe plum tomatoes, coarsely chopped
Salt and freshly ground pepper, to taste
2 cups fresh baby spinach leaves
4 tablespoons grated Parmesan cheese
5 basil leaves, torn into small pieces

1.   Bring a large pot of salted water to a boil. Add the pasta and cook according to package directions or until al dente, stirring occasionally. While the pasta is cooking, place the peas in a small strainer and blanch for 1 minute in the same pot of pasta water. Remove peas and drain.

2.   Meanwhile, add 1 tablespoon olive oil to a large nonstick skillet. Add the garlic and red pepper flakes and cook briefly, taking care not to brown the garlic. Add the tomatoes, salt, and pepper. Cook for 2 minutes over medium heat, stirring frequently.

3.   Add the drained pasta to the skillet. Add the peas, the remaining 1 tablespoon olive oil, and the spinach leaves and toss until spinach is wilted. Add the Parmesan and blend well. Sprinkle with basil leaves and serve immediately.

RISOTTO

—

YIELD: 4 SERVINGS

Risotto is traditionally made with butter, which I prefer. You can substitute olive oil if you like, or use a combination. This risotto is especially delicious when garnished with thin slices of white or black truffle. While in Italy I came upon a special risotto rice called riso superfino carnaroli, *which is a specialty of Parma. Its texture is a bit different from arborio and the grains are rounder. It can be found in specialty food shops in the United States.*

3 cups fresh or canned chicken broth
3 tablespoons butter
3 tablespoons finely chopped onion
1 tablespoon finely chopped garlic
1 cup raw arborio or carnaroli rice or converted rice
Salt and freshly ground pepper, to taste
1 cup dry white wine
4 tablespoons freshly grated Parmesan cheese

1. Heat the broth in a saucepan and keep it at a simmer.

2. Heat 1 tablespoon butter in a large, heavy saucepan over medium heat. Add the onion and garlic, and cook, stirring, until wilted; do not let the garlic brown. Add the rice and salt and pepper. Stir to coat the grains. Add the wine and cook, stirring occasionally, until all the wine has evaporated.

3. Add ¼ cup of the hot broth to the rice mixture and cook over low heat, stirring occasionally, until all the broth has been absorbed. Add another ¼ cup of the broth and cook, stirring occasionally, until all has been absorbed. Continue cooking the rice in this fashion until all the broth has been used. Remember that the rice must cook gently.

4. When the broth has been absorbed, fold in the remaining 2 tablespoons butter and the cheese. Blend well. When the rice is done, the grains should be tender except at the very core, which should retain a very small bite. The total cooking time should be 25-28 minutes for arborio rice; if converted rice is used, the cooking time should be a little less.

TORTELLINI WITH GROUND TURKEY AND RED WINE SAUCE

YIELD: 4 SERVINGS

In order to keep the fat content of this dish low, I have substituted ground turkey for ground beef or pork. I prefer to grind my own turkey, to ensure freshness. Turkey breasts are now available in most supermarkets. Remove the skin and bone, cut the meat into half-inch cubes, and chop coarsely in a food processor.

1 tablespoon olive oil

1 cup finely chopped onion

1 tablespoon finely chopped garlic

1 pound coarsely ground lean white turkey

Salt and freshly ground pepper, to taste

2 cups crushed Italian canned tomatoes

2 ounces prosciutto, chopped

½ cup dry red wine

⅛ teaspoon hot red pepper flakes

1 tablespoon chopped fresh basil

2 teaspoons chopped fresh oregano

½ teaspoon chopped fresh rosemary

1 pound fresh tortellini with cheese

Grated Parmesan cheese (optional)

1. Heat the oil in a large nonstick skillet over medium heat. Add the onion and garlic and cook, stirring, until wilted. Add the ground turkey and cook, chopping down and stirring with the side of a heavy metal spoon to break up the lumps, until the meat loses its raw color, about 5 minutes. Add salt and pepper. Drain away most of the fat, if necessary.

2. Add the tomatoes, prosciutto, wine, red pepper flakes, basil, oregano, and rosemary. Cook over moderately low heat for about 15 minutes.

3. Meanwhile cook the tortellini in boiling water according to package instructions or until tender. Do not overcook. Drain well.

4. Pour half of the simmering sauce over the tortellini and toss well. Serve with more sauce and some Parmesan cheese on the side.

BASIC POLENTA WITH CHEESE

YIELD: 4 SERVINGS

Polenta is a yellow cornmeal dish that is very popular in Italy, made in a variety of ways. The basic version is with water. From there, you can add different ingredients. In this recipe, I choose to add olive oil and some Parmesan cheese. Adjust the amount of cheese to your liking.

2 cups coarse-grain yellow cornmeal
2 tablespoons butter or olive oil
4 tablespoons freshly grated Parmesan cheese
Salt and freshly ground pepper, to taste

1. Bring 6 cups of salted water to a boil in a large, heavy pot. Gradually add the cornmeal, stirring, in a very thin stream. Keep stirring while simmering the cornmeal mixture for 20 minutes. The polenta is done when it pulls away from the side of the pot as you stir.

2. Add the butter or olive oil and a little more water if necessary to thin the mixture to the desired consistency. Add the cheese and salt and pepper, check for seasoning, and blend well. Serve promptly.

A fresh grating of Parmesan cheese tops the polenta.

PIERRE FRANEY
WITH

PAOLA &
MAURIZIO
CAVAZZINI

INTRODUCTION

*I*t's difficult to visit Parma with the intention of eating low-fat. Known the world over for its cheese and prosciutto, Parma also makes butter an integral part of its cuisine. Combine these ingredients with wonderful ripe tomatoes, a bit of garlic, homemade pasta, and a glass of Lambrusco, and you experience a gastronomic delight that is hard to turn down. So I was quite impressed when I visited Paola and Maurizio Cavazzini, the owners of La Greppia. They have found a way to incorporate all of the wonderful ingredients for which Parma is known in a cuisine that uses less fat.

Paola is the chef at La Greppia, overseeing a small kitchen staffed only with women, including her sisters. Maurizio runs the dining room. Paola's grandparents started the restaurant in 1908. She believes strongly in classical Italian cuisine, and her menu includes many of her grandparents' recipes, which are rich in butter and cheese. But she has also created dishes with a lower fat content, taking advantage of the local fresh produce.

She and Maurizio both demonstrated recipes in which the traditional butter was replaced with olive oil. They confirmed what other top chefs have said: only the freshest of ingredients achieve the most satisfying flavor.

LEFT: *A cheerful striped awning caps the entrance to La Greppia in Parma.* OVERLEAF: *The view of La Greppia's busy kitchen through a window in the dining room.*

PORK TENDERLOIN ROLLS WITH PROSCIUTTO

—

YIELD: 4 SERVINGS

Paola made delicious pork rolls stuffed with prosciutto and Parmesan cheese, Parma's specialties. They are easy to make, and you can substitute veal or turkey breast meat for the pork, if desired. Serve this with Mashed Potatoes with Olive Oil (see page 97).

4 3-ounce pieces center-cut pork tenderloin, trimmed of fat

4 thin slices prosciutto

4 ounces Parmesan cheese, shaved into thin slices

2 tablespoons chopped fresh rosemary

2 tablespoons olive oil

½ cup dry white wine

½ cup fresh or canned chicken broth

4 sprigs rosemary, for garnish

1. Preheat the oven to 400° F.

2. On a flat surface, lay out the pork slices and cover with a sheet of plastic wrap. Using a meat pounder or wooden mallet, pound the pork slices into paper-thin sheets like scaloppine. Remove the plastic wrap and move the slices close to each other.

3. Place a slice of prosciutto over each pork slice. Next, place 2 shavings of Parmesan and sprinkle with rosemary. Roll each pork slice into a long tube and, without squeezing the meat, tie firmly with butcher's twine at 1-inch intervals.

4. Heat the olive oil in an ovenproof nonstick skillet large enough to hold the 4 rolls in one layer. Add the pork rolls and sauté over medium-high heat until lightly brown on all sides, 4 to 5 minutes. Add the wine and bring to a boil. Pour in the chicken broth, cover, and place in the oven to bake for 10 minutes.

5. Remove pan from the oven and place on top of the stove. Cook, uncovered, over medium-high heat until the sauce is reduced by half. Remove the rolls, untie, and slice on a bias into ¼-inch pieces. Pour over the wine sauce and garnish each roll with a sprig of rosemary.

BAKED APPLES WITH RASPBERRIES AND GRAND MARNIER

YIELD: 4 SERVINGS

Maurizio cores the apples for this recipe with a tool called an apple corer, which leaves the apple whole. If an apple corer is not available, use a small sharp knife to cut a hole on each end of the apple, then use a small demitasse spoon to scoop out the remaining core. Take your time; it is important that the apples remain whole..

4 Golden Delicious apples, cored and left whole
¼ cup raisins
2 cups dry white wine
½ cup Grand Marnier
⅓ cup sugar
24 raspberries, for garnish
4 sprigs fresh mint, for garnish

1. Preheat the oven to 350° F.

2. Place the apples in a baking dish large enough to hold them snugly. Divide the raisins evenly among the apples to fill each core hole. Pour the wine and half the Grand Marnier over the apples, and sprinkle the sugar evenly over the top.

3. Bake in the oven for 1 hour, or until very tender. Baste regularly to achieve a nice golden brown glaze. Remove and pour over the remaining Grand Marnier. Let cool.

4. To serve, place 1 apple on each plate and spoon over the sauce. Garnish with the raspberries and mint sprigs.

OSSO BUCO MILANESE

—

YIELD: 6 SERVINGS

It is important that the veal shanks are cut from the back leg and not from the front because you'll get more meat and less bone. I recommend that you serve this dish with Risotto (see page 85).

6 meaty pieces veal shank (about 5 pounds total weight), cut across the marrow, each piece about 2 inches thick

Salt and freshly ground pepper, to taste

Flour, for dredging

2 tablespoons olive oil

1½ cups finely chopped onion

½ cup chopped celery

1 cup chopped carrots

2 tablespoons plus 1 teaspoon finely chopped garlic

½ teaspoon crushed dried marjoram

2 sprigs fresh thyme, or ½ teaspoon dried

1 bay leaf

1½ cups dry white wine

2 cups crushed Italian canned tomatoes

1 teaspoon finely grated lemon rind

2 teaspoons finely grated orange rind

¼ cup finely chopped flat-leaf parsley

1. Sprinkle the shanks with salt and pepper, dredge in flour, and shake off the excess flour.

2. Heat the oil in a heavy skillet or Dutch oven large enough to hold the veal shanks upright in one layer. Over medium-high heat, brown the veal all over, about 20 minutes.

3. Add the onions, celery, and carrots and cook, stirring, about 5 minutes. Add 2 tablespoons garlic, the marjoram, thyme, and bay leaf. Stir and add the wine. Cook about 1 minute, then add the tomatoes and salt and pepper. Cover and cook over medium heat about 1¼ hours or until done.

4. Blend the lemon and orange rinds and the remaining teaspoon of garlic. Sprinkle over the veal and stir to blend. Cover and cook 15 minutes longer. Before serving, skim off any fat, remove the bay leaf, and sprinkle with chopped parsley.

MASHED POTATOES WITH OLIVE OIL

—

YIELD: 4 SERVINGS

Instead of using butter to make mashed potatoes, I have substituted a small quantity of olive oil, which has no cholesterol. I include one garlic clove to add more flavor. But more garlic can be added if you love its pungent flavor.

1¼ pounds Yukon Gold or Idaho potatoes, peeled and cut into 4-inch cubes
1 garlic clove, peeled
Salt, to taste
1 cup milk
2 tablespoons olive oil
Freshly grated nutmeg, to taste
Freshly ground white pepper, to taste

1. Place the potatoes in a large saucepan and cover with cold water. Add the garlic and salt, bring to a boil, and simmer for 20 minutes or until the potatoes are tender. Do not overcook.

2. Meanwhile, heat the milk until hot.

3. Drain the potatoes and, along with the cooked garlic, put them through a food mill or ricer or mash with a potato masher. Return them to the saucepan and, using a wooden spatula, add the olive oil, nutmeg, and pepper. Blend well. Add the hot milk and blend again. Check for seasoning. Keep warm until ready to serve.

MUSSEL SOUP PARMA STYLE

YIELD: 4 SERVINGS

Europeans have always eaten mussels, and Americans are just starting to catch on. They are a good source of protein with little fat. It is important that you use fresh mussels. In some markets, the mussels are shelled, but I find these are tasteless and not as fresh. Serve this soup with Garlic Croutons (below).

4 tablespoons olive oil
1 tablespoon finely chopped garlic
1 cup finely chopped fennel
½ cup dry white wine
1 cup crushed Italian canned tomatoes
½ cup finely chopped basil or flat-leaf parsley
Salt and freshly ground pepper, to taste
¼-½ teaspoon hot red pepper flakes
5 pounds mussels (about 4 quarts), well scrubbed and
    beards removed

1. Heat the oil in a large heavy-bottomed pot. Add the garlic and fennel, and cook briefly until wilted. Do not brown. Add the wine and cook for 1 minute. Add the tomatoes, basil or parsley, salt, pepper, and red pepper flakes and simmer for 2 minutes.

2. Add the mussels, cover tightly, and cook, shaking the pot so they cook evenly, for 5 minutes or until the mussels are fully opened. Discard any mussels that have not opened. Ladle mussels and liquid into individual bowls and serve.

GARLIC CROUTONS

YIELD: 4 SERVINGS

These croutons go well with fish or onion soup. They can also be added to a salad—simply cut the toasted slices into half-inch cubes, add to the salad, and toss.

1 loaf crusty French or Italian bread, about 14 inches
    long
2 garlic cloves, peeled and cut in half
2 tablespoons olive oil
4 tablespoons freshly grated Parmesan cheese

1. Preheat the oven to 450° F.

2. Rub the loaf on all sides with the garlic cloves.

3. With a bread knife, cut slices about ¼ inch thick. Arrange the slices on a baking sheet, brush lightly with the olive oil, and sprinkle the tops evenly with the Parmesan cheese.

4. Place in the oven and bake about 10 minutes or until lightly browned on top.

BRAISED CABBAGE WITH PROSCIUTTO

YIELD: 4 SERVINGS

This side dish goes well with any version of roasted, baked, or sautéed pork. I blanch the cabbage before cooking it with the onions and garlic in order to remove any strong cabbage flavor.

1 head savoy or green cabbage
1 tablespoon olive oil
½ cup finely chopped onion
1 teaspoon chopped garlic
2 ounces lean prosciutto, cut into thin strips
2 whole cloves
1 teaspoon ground coriander
1 cup fresh or canned chicken broth
Salt and freshly ground pepper

1. Cut away and discard any tough core from the cabbage. Open up the leaves and remove any remaining tough ribs.

2. Bring a large pot of salted water to a boil. Add the cabbage; when the water returns to a boil, cook 5 minutes. Drain well.

3. Cut or chop the cabbage into 2-inch cubes.

4. Heat the olive oil in a large casserole or heavy skillet. Add the onion, garlic, and prosciutto. Cook, stirring, until wilted. Add the cabbage, cloves, and coriander. Add the broth, then season generously with salt and pepper. Bring to a boil, cover tightly, and cook over moderate heat for 10–15 minutes, or until the cabbage is done. Serve hot.

BROOK TROUT WITH LEMON AND CAPERS

YIELD: 4 SERVINGS

Personally, I prefer to cook fish with the heads on because it makes for a better presentation. Also, when purchasing a whole fish, I can check its freshness. The gills should be bright red and the eyes should be bright, not opaque.

4 fresh brook trout (about 10 ounces each), cleaned and
    preferably with heads on, scales removed

¼ cup low-fat milk

½ cup all-purpose flour

Salt and freshly ground pepper, to taste

2 tablespoons vegetable or corn oil

2 tablespoons olive oil

⅓ cup drained capers

1 lemon, peeled and cut into very small seedless cubes

2 tablespoons finely chopped parsley

1. Rinse each trout inside and out in cold water and pat dry. Using a pair of kitchen shears, cut off the fins. Place the trout in a dish and add the milk. Turn the fish to coat with the liquid. Remove the trout and dredge it in flour, then season with salt and pepper. Shake to remove the excess flour.

2. Heat the vegetable oil in a nonstick skillet large enough to hold the trout in one layer. Cook over moderately high heat about 4-5 minutes or until golden brown on one side. Turn and cook until golden brown on the other side. As the fish cooks, baste often with the oil in the skillet. Continue to cook until the trout are cooked through, turning occasionally so they cook evenly. Total cooking time is 10-15 minutes. Transfer the fish to a warm serving platter.

3. Pour off the fat from the skillet and wipe out if necessary. Heat the olive oil over medium-high heat, add the capers, and cook, stirring, until lightly browned. Add the lemon cubes, blend well, and pour over the trout. Sprinkle with chopped parsley.

Ziti with Mussels and Sugar Snap Peas

Yield: 4–6 servings

The mussels in this recipe are not cooked in any water. They are steamed in their own juices. Northern Italians do not, as a rule, serve Parmesan cheese with seafood pasta. I happen to disagree; I see no conflict. In this recipe, I leave the decision up to you.

2 pounds mussels, beards and barnacles removed, washed and drained well
2 sprigs fresh thyme, or ½ teaspoon dried
1 bay leaf
4 whole cloves
¾ pound sugar snap peas
¾ pound ziti or other tubular pasta
2 tablespoons olive oil
1 tablespoon finely chopped garlic
2 cups crushed Italian canned tomatoes
1 tablespoon fresh oregano, or ½ teaspoon dried
1 small jalapeño pepper, cored, seeded, and chopped
Salt and freshly ground pepper, to taste

1. Place the mussels in a saucepan with the thyme, bay leaf, and cloves. Tightly cover and cook over high heat, shaking the pan occasionally, for 3 minutes or until the mussels are opened. Remove the mussels with a slotted spoon and set aside to cool. Reserve the broth from the mussels and strain. Discard any mussels that have not opened. When the mussels are cool enough to handle, remove the meat and discard the shells.

2. Trim the ends of the peas and drop them in 2 quarts boiling water. When the water returns to a boil, cook 2-3 minutes. Do not overcook. Remove and set aside.

3. Add the ziti to the boiling water. Stirring occasionally, cook for about 9 minutes or to the desired degree of doneness. Do not overcook. Drain.

4. Meanwhile, heat 1 tablespoon of the olive oil in a large nonstick skillet. Add the garlic and cook briefly. Do not brown. Add the tomatoes and the reserved mussel cooking liquid, oregano, jalapeño pepper, salt, and pepper. Bring to a boil and simmer for 5 minutes.

5. Add the drained ziti and cook, stirring, for 2-3 minutes. Add the mussels, peas, and remaining 1 tablespoon olive oil. Toss and blend well while cooking briefly. Serve hot.

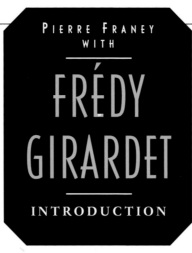

*I*n the small Swiss town of Crissier, located just north of Lausanne, is the *Guide Michelin* three-star restaurant of Frédy Girardet. I first met Frédy in 1976, when I was traveling through Europe on a tour of the continent's best restaurants for *The New York Times*. Frédy was the new big name on the restaurant scene. With a reputation as a chef who took *la nouvelle cuisine* to new heights, he had an uncanny ability to bring a delectable harmony to his dishes by combining a variety of flavors. He is still doing that today.

Restaurant Girardet is cited as one of the best restaurants in the world, and it is easy to see why. Frédy is a perfectionist in the kitchen as well as in the dining room, overseeing every plate before it is served. He also visits each table in the dining room, greeting his guests and making certain they are pleased. He believes that it is important to preserve the natural flavors of ingredients, and he is adamant about quality. For example, in the spring you will never find farm-raised salmon on his menu. In May and June, when the salmon are running, he has wild Scottish salmon flown in on a daily basis. For him, the meat is much firmer, of better quality, and therefore of better flavor.

Routine bores Frédy, and he is always thinking of new ways to prepare his dishes. He approaches each day with spon-

Restaurant Girardet's elegant façade.

taneity: the realities of the moment, the ingredients available, even the weather can influence the way he cooks. Although he is not averse to using cream and butter, he also takes care to make dishes that are not laden with fat. Frédy believes in the simple side of French cuisine. His sauces are not made with flour but, rather, are simple reductions of cooking juices. His soufflés contain no butter, no milk, and no flour. They are light and airy.

Frédy is also a great believer in exercise. He is a fit, trim man who keeps weight off by riding his bicycle many miles each day. He loves to ski in the wintertime. Coming from a modest background, he did not apprentice in the great and established kitchens. He worked in his father's bistro in Crissier as a young man, spent three years at a brasserie in Lausanne, and used his free time to play sports. Upon his father's death, he took over the family restaurant. Shortly thereafter, he took a trip to France and ate at the great kitchens of Pierre and Jean Troisgros and Paul Bocuse.

Frédy's vision for his restaurant was completely altered by his eating experiences there. His creative juices flowing, he went back to Crissier full of inspiration and the family bistro was soon transformed into a high-class restaurant.

ABOVE: *Exuberant grillwork announces the restaurant.* OPPOSITE: *Phillippe Rochat, second in command at Restaurant Girardet, with Frédy Girardet and Pierre.* OVERLEAF: *The Restaurant Girardet, housed in the former city hall of the village of Crissier.*

Frédy invited me into his kitchen and prepared two health-conscious recipes that appear on his menu: Wild Scottish Salmon with Sea Salt and Passion Fruit Soufflé. I noticed that in preparing the salmon, he brushed the surface with butter but was careful to remove the excess by blotting the fish with a paper towel. The fennel puree that accompanies the salmon has no butter added—it is made only of fennel and some of its reserved cooking juices. The soufflé, which is low in fat, has always been popular with the restaurant's diners. The flavor of passion fruit has an edge of tartness along with a hint of flowers. It is a perfect way to end a meal.

WILD SCOTTISH SALMON WITH SEA SALT

YIELD: 4 SERVINGS

Frédy Girardet is not a fan of raw salmon and has never served salmon carpaccio in his restaurant. But he created this recipe in the 1980s, during the "carpaccio craze." The salmon is lightly cooked at a low temperature until just lukewarm. Frédy uses only wild Scottish salmon, caught during the salmon fishing season in May and June, which are flown in daily from Scotland. Because wild salmon is rarely found in U.S. markets, the farm-raised variety can be easily substituted for home cooking. Sel de Guérande is a sea salt that comes from Brittany, France, which is widely used by European chefs.

1 very ripe, large plum tomato, peeled and seeded

Salt and freshly ground pepper, to taste

1 pound center-cut salmon fillet, skin on, scaled

3 small, young fennel bulbs, outer leaves removed, coarsely chopped (about 2 cups), some leaves reserved for garnish

1 red jalapeño pepper, cored, seeded, and finely chopped

2 tablespoons cleaned and finely diced baby leek

4 tablespoons extra-virgin olive oil

1 cup dry white wine

½ cup fish stock

½ teaspoon fresh lemon juice

3 tablespoons softened butter

1 tablespoon sea salt (preferably *Sel de Guérande*)

Freshly cracked white peppercorns

1. Preheat the oven to 325° F.

2. Prepare the tomato confit. Drop the tomato in boiling water for 10 seconds, then remove and let cool. Peel the tomato, core it, and then cut it into quarters lengthwise and remove the seeds so you are left with 4 tomato petals. Season well with salt and pepper and place in the oven for about 1 hour to dehydrate the tomato and intensify the flavor. Remove and cut into thin strips, then dice in ⅛-inch pieces. Set aside.

3. Remove 1 inch along the length from the thinner side of the salmon fillet to create a rectangle of even thickness. Divide into 4 equal portions. Reserve the leftovers for another recipe.

4. In the meantime, bring a large saucepan of salted water to a boil. Add the fennel, reduce the heat, and simmer 15 minutes, or until just tender. Drain, reserving ¼ cup cooking liquid, and remove to a food processor or blender. Puree well, adding reserved liquid, if necessary, to achieve a smooth texture, then push through a fine strainer. Transfer to a small saucepan and keep warm.

5. While the fennel is cooking, combine the jalapeño pepper with the baby leek, 2 tablespoons olive oil, and salt and pepper to taste in a small bowl. Set aside.

6. In a small saucepan, combine the wine and fish stock and bring to a boil. Continue to boil and reduce by two-thirds. Gradually whisk in the

remaining 2 tablespooons olive oil and emulsify with the sauce. Then whisk in the jalapeño pepper oil and diced tomato confit. Add the lemon juice and check for seasoning. Set aside.

7.   Brush a large, heavy enameled cast-iron baking dish lightly with half the butter and place the 4 salmon pieces skin side down. They should be at least 1½ inches apart. Season the fish with salt and pepper. Brush the flesh with the remaining butter and place a piece of foil loosely over the fish, just to cover but not to seal. Place in the oven and bake for 10 minutes or until lukewarm throughout. Do not overcook. Remove from the baking dish with a spatula to a separate plate, leaving all the fat behind. Remove the salmon skin and any dark meat that remains. Keep warm.

8.   To serve, reheat the fennel puree and place a pool of it in the center of the plate. Use a spoon to smooth the sauce out evenly. Leave a ¼-inch gap between the edge of the sauce and the rim of the plate. Fill in that gap with the jalapeño pepper sauce and place the salmon fillet in the center. Season the fillet with sea salt and white pepper. Garnish with fennel leaves.

PASSION FRUIT SOUFFLÉ

YIELD: 4 SERVINGS

This is a very light soufflé. Frédy has a unique way of making soufflés. Instead of putting the prepared soufflés directly in the oven, he begins to cook them on top of the stove in a bath of shallow, simmering water, or bain-marie. This helps the whipped egg whites to set and enables the soufflés to rise straight up and hold their shape. He finishes them in a very hot oven. For this recipe you'll need to chill two 2-cup soufflé molds.

Butter
8 whole ripe passion fruit or ¾ cup passion fruit juice
¾ cup superfine sugar
2 large egg yolks
4 large egg whites
Confectioners' sugar, for dusting

1. Preheat the oven to 400° F. Prepare a bain-marie or shallow saucepan large enough to hold the 2 soufflé molds side by side. Bring water to a boil in the bottom, then turn to a simmer.

2. Lightly butter the soufflé molds, coating the entire surface, then return molds to the refrigerator.

3. Cut the passion fruit in half and squeeze out the juice with an electric juicer or by hand. Strain. You should have ¾ cup.

4. Over high heat, bring ½ cup of the passion fruit juice to a boil in a small saucepan with ¼ cup of the sugar, whisking constantly. Lower the heat and simmer until syrupy and the sugar is dissolved. Remove and keep warm.

5. Place the egg yolks in a medium bowl and add ¼ cup sugar and ¼ cup passion fruit juice. Beat with a flexible wire whisk until the sugar is dissolved and the mixture thickens and is lemon-colored. When you lift the wire whisk, the mixture should form a ribbon.

6. Place the egg whites in a large mixing bowl. Add 2 tablespoons sugar and, with a large balloon whisk, begin to beat the whites. After they begin to foam, gradually add the remaining 2 tablespoons sugar and beat the whites until they form soft peaks.

7. Add ¼ cup of the egg whites to the egg yolk mixture and blend well. Then add the yolk mixture back into the whites, folding gently and quickly with a rubber spatula.

8. Spoon equal amounts of the prepared mixture into the 2 soufflé molds. The mixture should come to within ¼ inch of the top of the mold. Smooth the top and tap the molds on the counter to remove any air bubbles. Place the molds in the bain-marie of simmering water and warm over low heat on the top of the stove for 7 minutes. Then remove the molds and place on the bottom shelf of the oven to bake for an additional 6-7 minutes.

9. Serve the soufflés immediately, dusted with confectioners' sugar and with the sauce in a small sauceboat. Divide each soufflé between 2 plates and pour sauce over each portion.

LEMON CHICKEN

—

YIELD: 4 SERVINGS

In this recipe, I cook the chicken pieces with the skin on, because the skin keeps the meat moist. Before serving, I remove the skin to eliminate a lot of the fat. Boned skinless chicken breasts can also be used.

1 3½-pound chicken, cut into 10 serving pieces
Salt and freshly ground pepper, to taste
2 tablespoons olive oil
2 tablespoons finely chopped shallots
2 whole garlic cloves, peeled
8 lemon wedges, seeded
2 tablespoons lemon juice
¼ cup dry white wine
½ cup fresh or canned chicken broth
2 tablespoons chopped fresh coriander (cilantro) or parsley

1. Sprinkle the chicken on both sides with salt and pepper.

2. Heat 1 tablespoon olive oil in a heavy nonstick skillet large enough to hold the chicken pieces in one layer. When quite hot, add the chicken skin side down. Cook over medium-high heat until nicely browned, moving the pieces around, about 5 minutes.

3. Turn the chicken, and add the shallots and garlic. Cook about 2 minutes over medium-high heat. Drain off the fat, then add the lemon wedges, lemon juice, wine, and broth. Stir the bottom of the skillet with a wooden spoon to dissolve the brown particles that cling. Add the remaining tablespoon olive oil, cover, and simmer for about 10 minutes. Uncover the skillet and continue cooking until the sauce is reduced by half. Cover and cook for 10 minutes or until done.

4. Remove the chicken and take off the skin; keep warm. Cook the sauce over high heat until reduced by half. Return the chicken to the sauce and serve sprinkled with the coriander or parsley.

BAKED LOBSTER WITH BASIL STUFFING

YIELD: 4-8 SERVINGS

It is important that the lobsters are live when cut in half. Do not cut them too far in advance or you will lose all the juices. If you find this difficult to do, you may steam the whole lobsters very briefly before splitting them (see Note). Serve these lobsters with lemon wedges, Ginger Vinaigrette, or Light Tartar Sauce (see pages 47 and 69).

4 live lobsters (about 1½ pounds each)
4 tablespoons olive oil
2 tablespoons finely chopped shallots
¼ cup finely chopped onion
1 teaspoon finely chopped garlic
1½ cups fine fresh bread crumbs
¼ cup finely chopped fresh basil or flat-leaf parsley
Salt and freshly ground pepper, to taste

1. Preheat the oven to 500° F, or the highest setting on oven.

2. Insert a heavy knife into the lobster where the tail and the body meet to sever the spinal cord, killing the lobster instantly. Pull off the claws from each lobster, crack, and set aside. Split the lobster in half lengthwise. Discard the small tough sac near the eyes of each lobster. Arrange the lobster split side up in one layer in a baking dish. Combine the coral and the tomalley in a mixing bowl. Arrange the claws around the lobster.

3. Heat 1 tablespoon olive oil in a saucepan. Add the shallots, onion, and garlic. Cook, stirring, until wilted. Cool briefly.

4. Add the crumbs to the coral and tomalley mixture. Stir in the shallot and onion mixture. Add 2 tablespoons olive oil, the basil or parsley, salt, and pepper. Blend thoroughly.

5. Stuff the cavity of each lobster with an equal portion of the mixture. Brush the remaining tablespoon olive oil on the tail meat of the lobsters. Place the lobsters on the bottom rack of the oven. Bake for 15-20 minutes, or until done. Do not overcook.

NOTE: To steam the lobsters, bring about 2 inches of water to a rapid boil over high heat in the bottom of a steamer. Drop in the lobsters, cover, and cook for 1 minute—enough time to kill them quickly. Remove, split in half, and continue with the recipe.

Veal Chops with Vinegar Glaze

Yield: 4 servings

I first cooked this recipe as a young apprentice cook at Drouant in Paris, where the chef at the time was Emile Domas. I now make it with only 1 tablespoon of butter and 1 of olive oil. This small amount of butter, added at the end, binds the sauce and gives the dish a rich butter flavor. This dish can be served with Potato and Carrot Puree or Potatoes au Gratin (see pages 115 and 117).

4 loin veal chops (about ½ pound each), with most of the fat removed
Salt and freshly ground pepper, to taste
1 tablespoon olive oil
4 whole garlic cloves, peeled
2 small bay leaves
4 sprigs fresh thyme, or ½ teaspoon dried
1 tablespoon red wine vinegar
½ cup fresh chicken broth
1 tablespoon unsalted butter
2 tablespoons finely chopped parsley

1. Sprinkle the chops on both sides with salt and pepper.

2. Heat the olive oil in a large nonstick skillet. Over medium-high heat, brown the chops on both sides, turning once. They should cook about 5 minutes for each side.

3. Add the garlic, bay leaves, and thyme. Cook about 3 minutes, but do not let the garlic brown.

4. Drain the fat from the skillet. Pour the vinegar around the chops and turn the heat to medium high. Add the broth, cover tightly, and cook for about 15 minutes. Uncover to see if liquid has been reduced by half. Add the butter and cook about 3 minutes more or until sauce has a slightly thickened consistency.

5. Before serving, remove the thyme sprigs and bay leaves. The garlic cloves may be served on each plate. Sprinkle with chopped parsley.

POTATO AND CARROT PUREE

—

YIELD: 4 SERVINGS

The carrots and fresh coriander add a nice color and texture to this basic recipe for mashed potatoes. I cut out the butter completely and use only a small amount of olive oil to bind the mixture. Serve this delicious puree with any roast.

3-4 Idaho potatoes (about 1 pound)
4-6 large carrots (about ¾ pound)
½ cup sliced onion
Salt and freshly ground white pepper, to taste
1 tablespoon olive oil
½ cup warm whole milk
⅛ teaspoon freshly grated nutmeg
2 tablespoons finely chopped fresh coriander (cilantro)

1. Peel the potatoes and cut them into 2-inch cubes.

2. Trim the ends of the carrots, scrape them, and cut into 1-inch lengths. Place the potatoes, carrots, and onion in a large saucepan. Add water to cover and salt. Bring to a boil, then reduce heat and simmer for 20 minutes or until tender. Do not overcook or the vegetables will be watery and mushy.

3. Drain the potatoes and carrots, and push through a food mill or potato ricer. Return to the saucepan.

4. Add the white pepper and olive oil, and blend well with a wooden spatula. Place over low heat and add the warm milk gradually, blending with the spatula. Add the nutmeg and coriander, beating rapidly with a wooden spoon. Serve immediately.

MONKFISH AND SCALLOPS IN BOUILLABAISSE SAUCE

Monkfish used to be known as poor man's lobster. Years ago I would go to the beaches of eastern Long Island to watch the local fishermen pull in their nets. They picked the monkfish out of their morning catch and discarded them on the beach. I would quickly pick up the monkfish and bring them home to cook. Now monkfish is recognized for its delicate yet firm and lean meat, and its price has risen with its popularity. Serve this with rice or Garlic Croutons (see page 98).

1 tablespoon olive oil
½ cup finely chopped onion
¼ cup chopped leeks, white part only
½ cup chopped fennel
¼ cup chopped celery
4 small ripe plum tomatoes, peeled, seeded, and cut into small cubes
½ teaspoon saffron threads
1 cup fish stock or bottled clam juice
¼ cup dry white wine
1 bay leaf
2 sprigs fresh thyme, or ½ teaspoon dried
⅛ teaspoon Tabasco sauce
Salt and freshly ground pepper, to taste
4 small skinless monkfish fillets (about 4 ounces each)
¾ pound sea or bay scallops (cut sea scallops into quarters)
4 tablespoon chopped parsley

1. Heat the oil in a skillet large enough to hold the fish in one layer. Add the onion, leeks, fennel, and celery. Cook, stirring constantly, over medium heat until wilted; do not brown. Add the tomatoes, saffron, fish stock, wine, bay leaf, thyme, Tabasco, salt, and pepper. Cook over medium heat for about 10 minutes.

2. Add the monkfish and bring to a boil. Reduce the heat and simmer for 3 minutes. Add the scallops, cover, and simmer for 5 minutes more or until done. Take care not to overcook. Remove the bay leaf, sprinkle with parsley, and serve immediately.

POTATOES AU GRATIN

YIELD: 8-10 SERVINGS

These potatoes are traditionally made with milk and cream. Instead, I use chicken broth, which has almost no fat.

2½ pounds Idaho potatoes
1 tablespoon olive oil
2 cups sliced white onion
2½ cups fresh or canned chicken broth
1 bay leaf
⅛ teaspoon freshly grated nutmeg
Salt and freshly ground pepper, to taste
¼ cup Comté or Gruyère cheese, grated

1. Preheat the oven to 400° F.

2. Peel the potatoes and cut them into ⅛-inch slices with a slicer—they must be of uniform size. Place them in a mixing bowl with cold water to remove the starch. Drain thoroughly.

3. Rub the bottom of a large flameproof gratin dish with the oil and add the potatoes and onion. Spread out evenly. Pour the broth over the potatoes. Place the bay leaf in the center of the potatoes and sprinkle with several gratings of nutmeg. Season with salt and pepper. Bring to a boil on top of the stove. Turn off the heat and add the cheese, spreading it evenly over the top. Place in the oven for 40 minutes, or until lightly browned. Remove the bay leaf and serve.

SAUTÉED APPLES IN CALVADOS

YIELD: 4-6 SERVINGS

Make this dessert with your favorite variety of apple, and serve it with sherbet, ice cream, cake, or simply on its own.

2 pounds apples, such as Golden Delicious or McIntosh
½ cup sugar
1 tablespoon butter
¼ cup honey
⅛ teaspoon ground cinnamon
4 tablespoons Calvados
Banana Sherbet (see page 17)

1. Peel the apples and remove the cores. Cut each apple into 8 sections.

2. Heat the sugar in a large nonstick skillet over medium heat. Stir the sugar until it starts to caramelize. Immediately add the butter and honey, and stir to incorporate into the caramel. Quickly add the apples and cinnamon. In the beginning the apples will start to stick; add the Calvados, reduce the heat, and flame over low heat. Cook, stirring and spooning the sauce over the apples, until the alcohol burns off, about 6 minutes. When ready, the apple pieces should be tender but not mushy.

3. Serve immediately with scoops of Banana Sherbet on top of the apples.

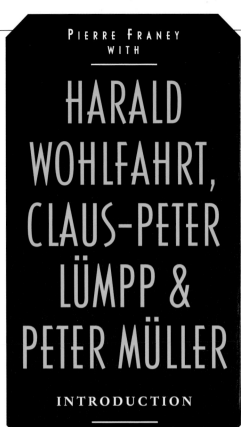

HARALD WOHLFAHRT, CLAUS-PETER LÜMPP & PETER MÜLLER

INTRODUCTION

*T*he Black Forest, in the southwest corner of Germany, is a magnificent area known for its thick pine and fir trees, mountain meadows, and bubbling mineral springs. It is a favorite vacation spot for people from around the world; in particular, the Germans themselves come here for lengthy stays or weekend retreats. Vigorous hikes, horseback rides, cycling, skiing, sailing, and windsurfing are just some of the activities that vacationers seek out when coming to the Black Forest. It is also a place known for its health spas, "cures," massages, and mud packs. Not surprisingly, it is considered the gastronomic center of Germany, with many wonderful restaurants in the small towns and villages throughout the region.

I visited and ate at two notable restaurants while traveling through the Black Forest. They are both located in grand full-ser-

Pierre enjoys a dance at this Bavarian tavern.

vice hotels and are, interestingly, near the same small resort town of Baiersbronn. Both are high-quality restaurants that are famous internationally because of their hardworking chefs, who trained in traditional German restaurants but whose style of cooking is not classically Germanic, with lots of sausages, wild game, and potatoes. Rather, their menus are influenced greatly by French cuisine, both chefs having spent some time working in kitchens in France. Because many of their diners are vacationers enjoying the spas and the healthier side of life, the chefs must plan menus that offer nutritious and light-tasting dishes.

Harald Wohlfahrt is the chef at Schwarzwald Stube, in the luxurious resort hotel Traube Tonbach. He has earned a Michelin three-star rating, one of only two restaurants in all of Germany to have that honor. Although he has spent little time outside of Germany, his style of cooking is predominantly French—with an emphasis on French produce and light, reduced sauces. The lush decor of the restaurant is German, with a carved wooden ceiling, plush armchairs, thick curtains, heavy wooden doors, and candelabra on the tables. Harald's menu includes some low-fat dishes for those of his clientele who are watching what they eat. When I asked him to prepare a low-fat dish for me, he chose to make Spicy Lobster, a preparation that shows a Japanese influence with its use of Japanese rice noodles, tree ear mushrooms, and soy sauce. A little olive oil is used in the cooking, but the rest of the ingredients

LEFT: *Pierre raises his glass to the sounds of the accordion player.* OPPOSITE TOP: *Pierre watches as Paul Müller trims white aspargus.* OPPOSITE BOTTOM: *Harald Wohlfahrt demonstrates his Spicy Lobster as Pierre looks on.* OVERLEAF: *A scenic view of the town of Baiersbronn.*

are vegetables, spices, and herbs. A teaspoon of curry powder gives the dish its "spicy" quality. This dish successfully shows off Harald's inventiveness.

Just across town is another grand resort, the Hotel Bareiss. Claus-Peter Lümpp is the executive chef, and he has brought two-star fame to the hotel's formal dining room, the Restaurant Bareiss. The cuisine here is more Germanic than that of Harald, and local specialties appear throughout the menu, but the influence is definitely French-Mediterranean. The dining room is elegantly designed with light-colored furniture, fresh flowers, and large windows that look out toward the Black Forest. Peter Müller, one of the Hotel Bareiss's talented young chefs, prepared two light dishes that show his Germanic and his French training. Pike, a freshwater fish, is wrapped in thinly sliced German bacon, sautéed quickly in a little olive oil, and served with waxy red potatoes and apple-flavored Bareiss Sauerkraut (pages 128 and 129). These are popular dishes with the hotel's health-conscious clientele.

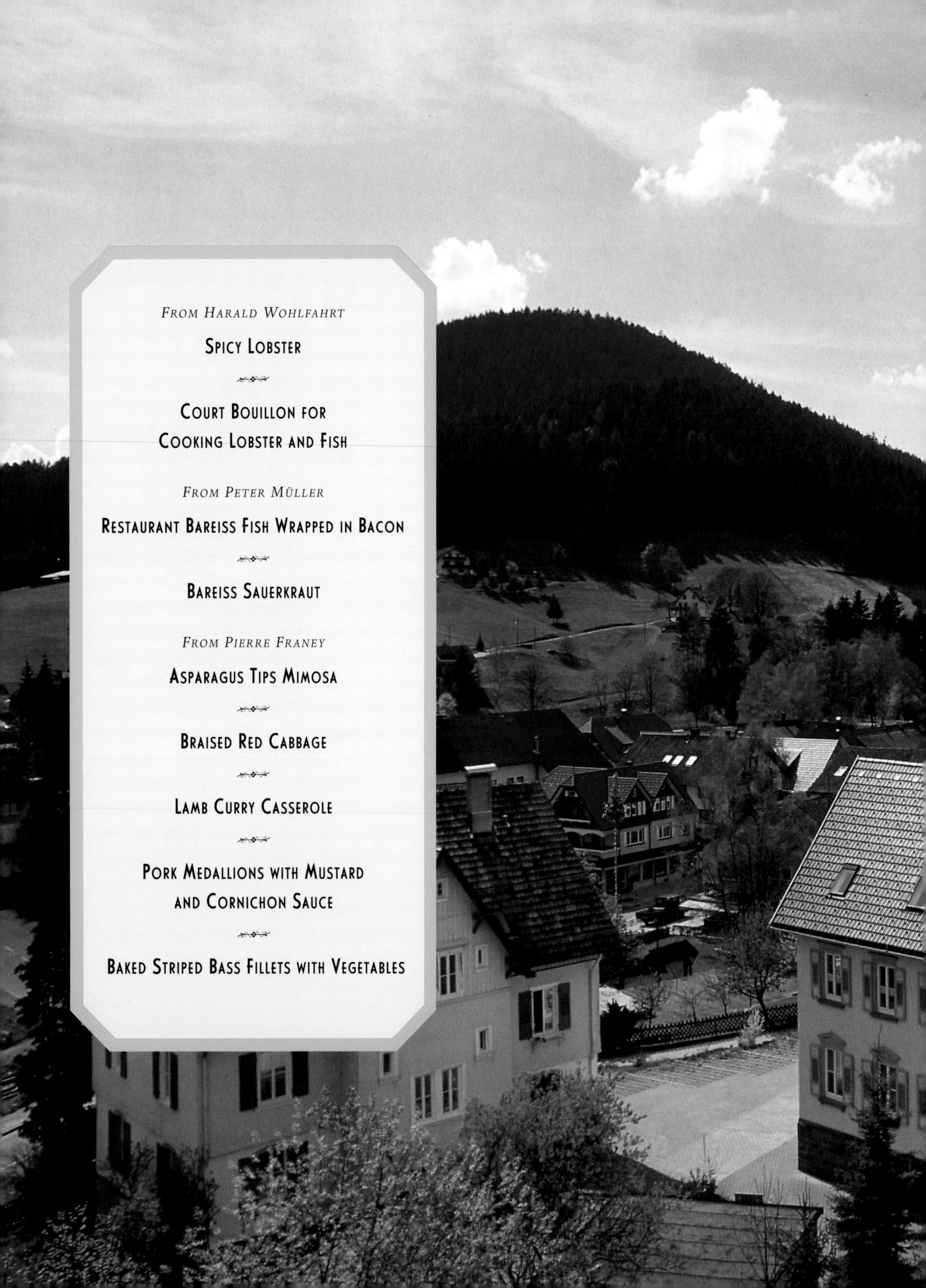

FROM HARALD WOHLFAHRT

SPICY LOBSTER

❧

COURT BOUILLON FOR
COOKING LOBSTER AND FISH

FROM PETER MÜLLER

RESTAURANT BAREISS FISH WRAPPED IN BACON

❧

BAREISS SAUERKRAUT

FROM PIERRE FRANEY

ASPARAGUS TIPS MIMOSA

❧

BRAISED RED CABBAGE

❧

LAMB CURRY CASSEROLE

❧

PORK MEDALLIONS WITH MUSTARD
AND CORNICHON SAUCE

❧

BAKED STRIPED BASS FILLETS WITH VEGETABLES

SPICY LOBSTER

—

YIELD: 4 SERVINGS

Each day, in his dining room at the Hotel Traube Tonbach, Harald Wohlfahrt prepares a nutritious and healthy dish for his spa clients. This Spicy Lobster is first cooked in a court bouillon, then the lobster meat is removed from the shell and sautéed until lightly browned. The accompanying vegetables and sauce give a Japanese flair to the dish.

Court Bouillon (see recipe following)

4 live 1¼-pound lobsters

¼ cup olive oil

1 cup cored, seeded, and julienned red bell pepper, in 2-inch strips

1 cup cored, seeded, and julienned yellow bell pepper, in 2-inch strips

1 cup soybean sprouts, trimmed of root

2 cups slivered light green part of leek, in 2-inch strips

1 cup Japanese rice noodles, blanched in boiling water for 1 minute

1 cup dried tree ear mushrooms, soaked 2 hours in warm water and drained well

Salt and freshly ground pepper, to taste

1 teaspoon curry powder

½ cup light soy sauce

1 tablespoon coarsely chopped fresh coriander (cilantro)

1. Bring the court bouillon to a boil in a large pot and add the lobsters. After the liquid has returned to a boil, reduce the heat and simmer for 3 minutes. Immediately remove the lobsters to an ice bath to cool. When they can be handled easily, remove from the ice bath to a tray. Remove only the claws (not the knuckle shell), and return the claws to the court bouillon to simmer for an additional 2 minutes. When the claws are ready, remove to the ice bath and cool. Strain and reserve ¼ cup of the court bouillon.

2. Over a large metal tray, crack the claw shells and remove the meat. Using a strong pair of scissors, cut along the edge of the knuckle shells and remove the knuckle meat in one piece; reserve. Separate the head from the tail, and split the head in half using a heavy knife and taking care to catch all the juices. Scrape away all the tomalley, taking care also to discard the hard bitter sack inside the head. Slice the tail straight through the shell into 4 rings, leaving 2 inches at the tail of the lobster. Slice the end of the tail lengthwise in half. Reserve all the lobster juices. Repeat for each lobster. Keep warm. Place all the shells and the juices from the cracked lobsters in a strainer, then strain and reserve. There should be about 1 cup of lobster juice.

3. Heat 2 tablespoons olive oil in a medium nonstick skillet over medium-high heat. Add the peppers and bean sprouts, leek, rice noodles, and mushrooms. Season with salt and pepper, then sauté quickly until wilted. Add the curry powder and soy sauce, and sauté briefly over high heat. Add the cooking juices from the lobster, bring to a boil, and remove skillet from heat. Keep warm.

(continued)

— 125 —

4. Place the remaining 2 tablespoons olive oil in a large nonstick skillet over medium-high heat. Add the lobster medallions and tail, and cook until browned on one side, then turn about one minute on each side. Add the claws and knuckle meat. Sauté until warm.

5. To serve, place the medallions of lobster around a warmed serving plate. Spoon the vegetables over and around the lobster. Add the strained court bouillon to the lobster pan and bring to a boil. Check for seasoning and spoon over the lobster and vegetables. Garnish with coriander.

COURT BOUILLON FOR COOKING LOBSTER AND FISH

———

YIELD: 2 QUARTS

This is a good basic court bouillon that can be used to poach any kind of fish.

½ cup sliced carrots, in ¼-inch-thick pieces
1 bulb fennel, sliced into ¼-inch-thick pieces
1 leek, green part only, coarsely chopped
2 sprigs thyme
1 bay leaf
5 white peppercorns
1 cup dry white wine
1 garlic clove
4 sprigs parsley
Salt, to taste

Place all the ingredients in a stockpot, add 2 quarts of water, and bring to a boil. Reduce the heat and simmer for 15-20 minutes. Strain before using.

RESTAURANT BAREISS FISH WRAPPED IN BACON

YIELD: 4 SERVINGS

The German bacon used in this recipe is very lean and helps to keep the fish moist while cooking. It also gives the fish a slight smoky flavor, which is very pleasant and goes very well with the sauerkraut. This bacon may be found in German specialty food markets. If you can't find it, look for very lean bacon, well trimmed of fat.

20 small waxy red potatoes

8 very thin slices German bacon

8 3-ounce fillets northern pike, catfish, or flounder, with no skin

Salt and freshly ground pepper, to taste

1 teaspoon olive oil

Bareiss Sauerkraut (see recipe following)

¼ cup chopped parsley

1.   Place the potatoes in a large pot and add enough salted water to cover. Bring to a boil, reduce heat, and simmer gently until tender, 15-20 minutes. Do not overcook. Remove and peel.

2.   While the potatoes are cooking, prepare the fish. Lay the bacon slices flat on a cutting board. Place 1 piece of fish, skin side up, centered on top of each slice of bacon. Trim the bacon so that it will wrap the fish in a single layer. Bring each side of the bacon around the fish to encircle it in one band, with the seam from the bacon on the outer side of the fish. Season with salt and pepper.

3.   Place the oil in a large nonstick skillet over medium heat. Lay the wrapped fish fillets in the skillet with the seam side of the bacon facing up. Cook 2-3 minutes, or until nicely browned. Turn the fish and continue cooking for an additional 3 minutes, or until nicely browned.

4.   Place a mound of sauerkraut, about 1 cup, in the center of each plate. Place 2 pieces of fish on top of each mound. Place 5 potatoes around each serving and sprinkle with parsley.

BAREISS SAUERKRAUT

YIELD: 4 SERVINGS

The fresh sauerkraut in Germany is delicious. It is crunchy, lightly salted, and, unlike sauerkraut found in the United States, it doesn't have to be soaked in water before using. Sauerkraut is low in calories but high in sodium, which can be reduced by rinsing in cold water. By adding a sliced apple, Peter Müller gives the sauerkraut a delicate sweetness.

2 tablespoons olive oil

1 medium onion, finely sliced

¼ cup dry white wine

1½ cups fresh or canned chicken broth

1 Golden Delicious apple, peeled, cored, divided into 8 sections, and sliced finely

Salt and freshly ground pepper, to taste

Pinch of sugar

4 cups drained fresh sauerkraut

1. Place the olive oil in a large nonstick skillet over medium heat. Add the onion and cook gently, not allowing the onion to brown, until wilted. Add the wine and broth and bring to a boil. Add the apple, season with salt, pepper, and a pinch of sugar, and reduce to a simmer. Loosely sprinkle the sauerkraut over the mixture, cover, and simmer 45 minutes, stirring occasionally.

Restaurant Bareiss Fish Wrapped in Salmon (page 127) with Bareiss Sauerkraut.

ASPARAGUS TIPS MIMOSA

YIELD: 4 SERVINGS

There are two kinds of cultivated asparagus—white and green. The white asparagus are popular in Europe while the green are common in the United States. Though the same plant, they are grown differently. White asparagus are covered with soil and, without sunlight, remain pale as they grow; green asparagus grow above the ground and turn green when exposed to the sun. They are similar in taste, although white asparagus tend to be a bit milder. Personally, I prefer green asparagus. Serve this as a first course or as a side dish with poached fish.

24 asparagus spears
1 hard-cooked egg
2 tablespoons olive oil
Salt and freshly ground pepper, to taste
1 tablespoon fresh lemon juice
2 tablespoons finely chopped chives or parsley

1. Line up the spears so the tips are in a straight line. Cut off the tough bottoms neatly to make them into equal lengths. Scrape the sides of each spear with a swivel-bladed paring knife, starting downward about 1½ inches from the tips.

2. Bring enough water to a boil in a large pot so that the spears are completely covered and add salt. Add the asparagus. Cook for about 1½ minutes, depending on the size of the asparagus; do not overcook. Drain and set aside.

3. Peel the egg and push it through a fine sieve, grate it with a fine grater, or chop it very finely.

4. Heat the oil in a small skillet, and when hot, add the egg and cook over high heat. Add salt, pepper, and lemon juice, shaking the skillet for about 30 seconds. Pour this over the asparagus, sprinkle with chives or parsley, and serve.

BRAISED RED CABBAGE

YIELD: 4 SERVINGS

Red cabbage is a fixture of German and Alsatian cooking. Its ruby red color makes for a nice presentation on the plate. In this version, I add a cup of orange juice to maintain the color and to add sweetness.

1 medium head red cabbage (about 2 pounds)

1 tablespoon olive oil

½ cup finely chopped onion

1 cup peeled, cored, and chopped apple

1 whole clove

¼ teaspoon ground allspice

Salt and freshly ground pepper, to taste

1 cup fresh orange juice or reconstituted frozen juice with pulp

2 tablespoons red wine vinegar

1. Quarter and core the cabbage; shred it finely.

2. Heat the olive oil in a large saucepan. Add the onion and cook over medium-high heat, stirring, until wilted. Add the apple, cabbage, clove, allspice, salt, and pepper. Cook, stirring, for 5 minutes. Add the orange juice and vinegar and bring to a boil. Cover, reduce the heat, and simmer, stirring occasionally, for 20 minutes. Most of the moisture should have evaporated. Serve hot.

Traditional Bavarian costumes of the Black Forest.

LAMB CURRY CASSEROLE

—

YIELD: 8-10 SERVINGS

Although curry is thought of as an Indian flavor, it is now found in all kinds of cuisines throughout Europe. When buying the lamb, be sure that the meat comes from the leg, because it will have less fat than meat from the shoulder or breast. And it is easy to remove the gristle because it is exposed and not in the meat or between bones. This curry can be served with a dab of plain yogurt on top. Rice and chutney are good accompaniments.

5 pounds boneless lamb from the leg, trimmed of fat

2 tablespoons vegetable oil

1 cup finely chopped onion

1 cup finely chopped celery

1 cup chopped peeled apple

1 cup chopped peeled banana

2 garlic cloves, minced

Salt and freshly ground pepper to taste

¼ cup curry powder, or to taste

2 tablespoons all-purpose flour

1 cup peeled, diced ripe tomatoes

1½ cups fresh or canned chicken broth

1 bouquet garni consisting of 4 sprigs fresh thyme, 1 bay leaf, and 6 sprigs parsley tied together

1 tablespoon chopped fresh coriander (cilantro)

1. Preheat the oven to 400° F.

2. Cut the lamb into 1½-inch cubes. Heat the oil in a large ovenproof skillet, Dutch oven, or casserole and add the lamb. Cook over medium-high heat, turning the pieces until lightly browned, for about 5 minutes. Drain the fat and add the onion, celery, apple, banana, garlic, and salt and pepper. Stir until most of the moisture evaporates.

3. Sprinkle with the curry powder and flour. Stir until the lamb is well coated. Add the tomatoes, broth, and bouquet garni. Bring to a boil and scrape the bottom with a wooden spatula. Cover and place in the oven for 1½ hours, or until the lamb is thoroughly tender.

4. Remove from the oven and spoon off any fat that may have risen to the top. Check for seasoning and sprinkle each serving with coriander.

PORK MEDALLIONS WITH MUSTARD AND CORNICHON SAUCE

YIELD: 4 SERVINGS

This recipe requires that the pork medallions marinate for a short time before cooking. This helps both to tenderize the meat and to flavor it. These medallions go well with Mashed Potatoes with Olive Oil and Braised Red Cabbage (see pages 97 and 130).

8 boneless pork loin slices with all fat removed (about 3 ounces each)
2 tablespoons olive oil
1 tablespoon lemon juice
1 tablespoon chopped fresh rosemary, or 2 teaspoons dried
⅛ teaspoon hot red pepper flakes
2 teaspoons ground cumin
Salt and freshly ground pepper, to taste
½ cup finely chopped onion
1 teaspoon finely chopped garlic
1 tablespoon red wine vinegar
½ cup fresh or canned chicken broth
1 tablespoon tomato paste
1 bay leaf
½ cup cornichons or sour gherkins, finely sliced
1 tablespoon Dijon mustard

1. Pound the pork slices on a flat surface but do not break the fibers. Place in a flat-bottomed, nonreactive dish large enough to accommodate the slices in one layer. Blend 1 tablespoon of the oil, the lemon juice, rosemary, red pepper flakes, cumin, salt, and pepper in a small bowl and brush on both sides of the slices. Let marinate 10-15 minutes.

2. In a nonstick skillet or a cast-iron pan large enough to hold all the pieces in one layer, heat the remaining tablespoon olive oil over medium-high heat. Add the pork slices and cook for about 10 minutes or until fully cooked, turning often until they become lightly browned. Do not overcook or the medallions will be dry. Remove to a warm platter.

3. Leaving the fat in the pan, add the onion and garlic and cook until wilted. Add the vinegar and cook briefly. Add the broth, tomato paste, and bay leaf. Reduce the heat and simmer for 5 minutes. Add the cornichons and swirl in the mustard. Return the pork medallions to the pan along with any juices that have accumulated. Blend well. Remove the bay leaf, baste the medallions with the sauce, and serve.

BAKED STRIPED BASS FILLETS WITH VEGETABLES

YIELD: 4 SERVINGS

In this recipe, the vegetable sauce can be made ahead of time and reheated just before cooking the fish. The fish, however, should be cooked just before serving. Other fish fillets such as red snapper or mahimahi can also be prepared this way.

2 tablespoons olive oil

1 cup chopped onion

2 teaspoons finely minced garlic

1 medium eggplant (about ½ pound), peeled and cut into ½-inch cubes

1 large red bell pepper, cored, seeded, and cut into small strips

4 ripe plum tomatoes (about ½ pound), seeded and cut into small cubes

1 tablespoon grated fresh ginger

½ cup dry white wine

Salt and freshly ground pepper, to taste

¼ cup coarsely chopped fresh coriander (cilantro), basil, or parsley

4 striped bass fillets with skin on (about 6 ounces each)

¼ cup fresh lime juice

1. Preheat the oven to 450° F.

2. Heat 1 tablespoon of the olive oil in a large skillet over medium-high heat. Add the onion and garlic and cook, stirring, until wilted. Add the eggplant, red pepper, tomatoes, and ginger. Cook, stirring, for about 5 minutes, then add the wine, salt, and pepper. Stir in the coriander, cover tightly, bring to a boil, reduce the heat, and simmer about 10 minutes.

3. Place the remaining tablespoon olive oil in a baking dish large enough to hold the fish in one layer. Arrange the fish skin side down in the dish, and sprinkle with salt, pepper, and lime juice. Spoon the sauce over and around the fish. Bake for 10 minutes, then test for doneness by piercing the center of fish with the tip of a sharp paring knife. The meat should be white and flaky, yet moist.

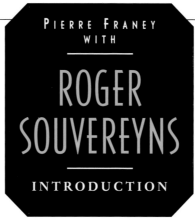

PIERRE FRANEY
WITH

ROGER
SOUVEREYNS

INTRODUCTION

*I*magine spending a weekend in the peaceful Flemish countryside in a renovated eighteenth-century farmhouse filled with carefully selected antiques, surrounded by lovely formal herb and flower gardens, and dining on tantalizing dishes cooked with special care by an accomplished chef and served on the finest porcelain. It sounds like a dream, but it is indeed a reality.

It is Scholteshof, the country inn and restaurant of Roger Souvereyns, one of Belgium's most innovative and talented chefs. Apprenticed at the age of fourteen in a restaurant in the Liège, he learned the basic principles of French cooking and went on to work in several restaurants in Belgium before opening three of his own. During that time he and his wife, Walda, became avid and expert collec-

RIGHT: *Pierre with Roger Souvereyns in the kitchen at Scholteshof, in front of the restaurant's 165-year-old stove.* OPPOSITE: *A stand of plane trees in the nearby Belgian countryside.*

ABOVE: *A canapé provides comfortable seating in the outdoor dining room at Scholteshof.* OVERLEAF: *A colorful display of Roger and Walda Souvereyns's collection of antique plates. Included are* barbotines, *special dishes for asparagus and artichokes.*

tors of antiques. In 1983, they bought an old, run-down farmhouse built in 1742, about 50 miles east of Brussels in the province of Limburg. Here they brought all their ideas, dreams, and passions together under one roof, seeking a perfect harmony of gastronomy and *savoir-vivre*—the art of living.

The farmhouse, located on 40 acres of country land, has been renovated with the greatest of care. Antique furniture; marble floors; paneled ceilings; sixteenth-century Flemish paintings depicting food, cooking, and eating; collections of antique plates, including one set of marvelous green ceramic asparagus serving plates; candles on all the tables; bouquets of flowers—every detail is carefully laid out. The overall effect is warm and charming. Overnight accommodations are spacious and beautifully furnished. Outside there are several gardens, one with more than eighty-five different herbs; an immense, perfectly manicured vegetable garden; flower gardens; and vineyards in the distance. Roger visits his gardens daily and cooks with what he himself picks. Local produce is an important part of his menu. For example, Belgian endive, grown on a local farm, are delivered to him daily.

Roger and his kitchen crew work in a large, airy kitchen that opens onto one of his three dining rooms. They work seriously and silently side by side, dressed all in white but without the traditional chef's hats. Roger personally cooks and oversees every dish that is served to his clients. His crew helps with the preparations. Everything is prepared to order on a 165-year-old range, which he found in a château and had converted to gas. One of Roger's unusual interests is his passion for antique spoons. He finds something sensual about them—round and perfect, an eating tool that holds flavors, aromas, and warmth in one place. Diners in his restaurant are served their appetizers on lovely large antique silver spoons, the food delicately laid out.

Roger cooks with ingredients of the very best quality in order to discover their true taste. Nyritol, a monosaturated oil with no cholesterol that a Belgian friend of his is developing, is used in his cooking because it is neutral in taste. He also believes in preparing food simply in order to preserve its natural flavors. A healthy, trim man, Roger is conscious of the need to watch the fat content of what he serves. During my visit, he invited me into his kitchen to watch him prepare Belgian Endive with Sea Scallops (see page 140). The endive were from a local farm, and the sea scallops were flown in from Scotland that morning. It is a light dish and quickly prepared.

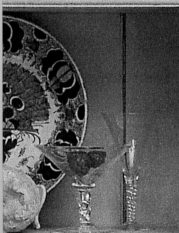

FROM ROGER SOUVEREYNS

BELGIAN ENDIVE WITH SEA SCALLOPS

❧

CHOCOLATE BEIGNETS WITH ORANGE COULIS

❧

FROM PIERRE FRANEY

FISH SOUP

❧

SAUTÉED CHICKEN WITH WINE AND HERBS

❧

SAUTÉED LAMB CHOPS WITH CUMIN

❧

STEAK WITH SHALLOT SAUCE

❧

LIGHT MEATBALLS WITH YOGURT SAUCE

❧

BOW TIE PASTA WITH GOAT CHEESE

❧

SUGAR SNAP PEAS WITH CARROTS

❧

NEW BITTERSWEET CHOCOLATE SORBET

BELGIAN ENDIVE WITH SEA SCALLOPS

YIELD: 4 SERVINGS

The key to making this recipe quickly is to prepare the ingredients ahead of time— the cooking time is minimal. The scallops are sautéed in a very hot, greaseless cast-iron skillet. It is important that you remove the scallops from the refrigerator about 15 minutes before cooking so they are not too cold. Test the scallops for doneness by piercing with the point of a knife; the meat should be white and moist. For a garnish, Roger Souvereyns went to his garden and picked geranium petals, but tarragon or any green herb may also be used.

4 large unblemished Belgian endive

Sea salt and freshly ground white pepper, to taste

4 tablespoons olive oil

1 Granny Smith apple, peeled, cored, quartered, and finely sliced

1 teaspoon honey

2 teaspoons apple cider vinegar

20 large sea scallops of uniform size

¼ cup geranium petals or tarragon leaves

1. Slice the endive across into 1-inch lengths and separate the leaves. You should have about 8 cups. Season with salt and pepper.

2. Place 2 tablespoons of the oil in a large nonstick skillet over high heat. Add the endive and sauté quickly, until lightly browned. Add the apple and continue to sauté until browned and nicely caramelized. Add the honey and vinegar to the pan and toss well. Taste and adjust the seasoning.

3. Season the scallops with salt and pepper. Over a high heat, heat a heavy cast-iron skillet large enough to hold the scallops in one layer. Dip the scallops in the remaining 2 tablespoons oil and place in the skillet. Cook until brown on both sides, 1-1½ minutes on each side, depending on the thickness. Do not overcook.

4. Divide the endive among 4 plates and place as a mound in the center of each plate. Place 5 scallops around the edges of each plate and sprinkle with the geranium petals or tarragon.

CHOCOLATE BEIGNETS WITH ORANGE COULIS

—

YIELD: 4 SERVINGS

I cannot really call this a low-fat dessert, but it is one of Roger's most popular ones, a signature dish and quite delicious.

1 quart peanut or vegetable oil, for frying

FOR THE GANACHE:

¾ cup heavy cream
5⅓ tablespoons (⅓ cup) butter
4 ounces semisweet Belgian chocolate

FOR THE BATTER:

¾ cup all-purpose flour
¼ cup unsweetened cocoa powder
2 tablespoons sugar
⅛ teaspoon salt
5⅓ tablespoons (⅓ cup) butter, softened
1 large egg
½ cup Champagne

FOR THE ORANGE COULIS:

1 cup fresh orange juice, unstrained
1 teaspoon orange blossom or other honey
½ cup sugar
¼ cup Grand Marnier

Fresh mint leaves, for garnish

1. In a deep fryer, heat the oil to 375° F and maintain at constant heat.

2. Combine the ganache ingredients in a small saucepan and place over low heat. Allow to melt, then mix well. Refrigerate for 15 minutes, or until firm enough to scoop up with a spoon. Place in a pastry bag with a medium tip.

3. In a large mixing bowl, combine the flour, cocoa, sugar, and salt. Add the butter and egg and combine well. Add the Champagne and mix until a smooth batter is formed.

4. To make the coulis: Combine the orange juice, honey, and sugar in a small saucepan over medium heat. Bring to a boil and let simmer until reduced by half. Strain and add the Grand Marnier. Allow to cool.

5. With the pastry bag, pipe 8 balls of the ganache 1½ inches in diameter onto a plate.

6. With 2 forks, lift a ball of ganache, dip it into the batter, and coat well. Lift it out and drop into the hot oil, leaving a trail of the batter behind. Remove from the oil when it begins to float, about 3 minutes, and place on a paper towel. Repeat with the remaining balls, cooking no more than 4 beignets at a time. Keep warm in a low oven until ready to serve.

7. Spoon orange coulis around the edge of each plate. Stand up 2 beignets in the center and garnish with fresh mint.

FISH SOUP

—

YIELD: 4 SERVINGS

One of my favorite summer pastimes is fishing in Peconic Bay, off Long Island, New York. I often make this fish soup for my family. Years ago I would have added cream and butter at the end to make a rich soup, but now I prefer it this way. I advise you to prepare the ingredients in advance—there is much chopping to be done.

2 tablespoons olive oil

½ cup chopped onion

1 tablespoon finely chopped garlic

½ cup finely chopped fennel

½ cup coarsely chopped leek

1 red bell pepper, cored, seeded, and cut into ½-inch cubes

1 cup diced carrots, in ¼-inch cubes

1 jalapeño pepper, cored, seeded, and finely chopped

½ teaspoon saffron threads

4 sprigs fresh thyme, or 2 teaspoons dried

1 bay leaf

2 cups fish stock or water

1 cup dry white wine

4 ripe plum tomatoes, seeded and cut into ½-inch cubes

Salt and freshly ground pepper, to taste

1½ cups diced skinless white-fleshed nonoily fish fillets, such as monkfish, tilefish, or cod, in 1-inch cubes

1 cup sea scallops, cut in half if large

¼ cup chopped fresh basil or parsley

Garlic Croutons (see page 98)

1.　Heat 1 tablespoon of the oil in a large saucepan over medium heat. Add the onion, garlic, fennel, leek, red pepper, and carrots. Cook, stirring often, over medium-high heat until the mixture is wilted. Do not brown.

2.　Add the jalapeño pepper, saffron, thyme, bay leaf, fish stock, wine, tomatoes, salt, and pepper. Bring to a boil, reduce the heat, cover, and simmer for 15 minutes.

3.　Add the fish and scallops, check for seasoning, and simmer 3 minutes. Do not overcook. Remove the bay leaf and thyme. Add the remaining tablespoon olive oil and the basil. Blend well. Serve immediately with the croutons.

SAUTÉED CHICKEN WITH WINE AND HERBS

—

YIELD: 4 SERVINGS

This is one of my favorite chicken recipes, one I learned as an apprentice cook in Paris. I have been making it ever since. But now I make it using olive oil and less butter. Also, I use the cooked garlic cloves to help bind the sauce at the end and to give it more flavor.

1 small chicken (3-3½ pounds), cut into serving pieces
Salt and freshly ground black pepper, to taste
1 tablespoon olive oil
2 garlic cloves, unpeeled
2 sprigs fresh thyme, or ½ teaspoon dried
1 large bay leaf
⅓ cup dry white wine
1 tablespoon butter

1.   Sprinkle the chicken with salt and pepper. To facilitate cooking, make a gash on each thigh opposite the skin side.

2.   Heat 1 tablespoon olive oil in a large, heavy skillet. When quite hot, add the chicken pieces, skin side down. Do not add the liver. Cook 5-7 minutes, or until golden brown, moving the pieces around to keep them from sticking. Turn the pieces, and add the garlic, thyme, and bay leaf.

3.   Add the liver and reduce the heat. Cook chicken over moderate heat, turning the pieces so they cook evenly, for 17-18 minutes.

4.   Remove the chicken to a warm platter, leaving the herbs in the pan. Carefully pour off the fat from the pan. Return the pan to the heat and add the wine. Cook over high heat, stirring to dissolve brown particles that cling to the pan, until the wine is reduced by half. Add ⅓ cup water and bring to a boil, then reduce by about half.

5.   Swirl in the butter. With a fork, squash the garlic cloves to squeeze out the softened insides. Remove the skins and blend the garlic puree with the sauce. Add the chicken pieces and any juices that have accumulated. Check for seasoning, remove the bay leaf, and serve.

SAUTÉED LAMB CHOPS WITH CUMIN

—

YIELD: 4 SERVINGS

I love the flavor of cumin, and it goes particularly well with lamb chops, giving them a nice golden brown color. Serve these chops with rice or potatoes.

8 rib lamb chops (3 ounces each), cut preferably from the rack, fat trimmed
Salt and freshly ground pepper, to taste
2 teaspoons ground cumin
4 plum tomatoes (about ¼ pound), peeled
2 tablespoons olive oil
1 teaspoon finely chopped garlic
¼ cup dry white wine
2 sprigs fresh thyme, or ¼ teaspoon dried
2 tablespoons finely chopped parsley

1. Sprinkle the lamb chops with salt and pepper and rub the cumin on both sides. Cut the tomatoes into small cubes; there should be about 1½ cups.

2. Heat 1 tablespoon of the olive oil in a large, heavy nonstick skillet and add the chops in one layer without crowding. Cook over high heat for 5 minutes and turn, then cook on the second side over medium-high heat. Cook 2-3 minutes for medium rare.

3. Remove the chops to a warm platter and pour off most of the fat. Return the skillet to the heat. When hot, add the garlic and stir, taking care not to burn it. Add the wine, tomatoes, salt, pepper, and thyme. Cook for a few minutes, then add any liquid that may have accumulated around the chops. Swirl in the remaining tablespoon olive oil. Divide the sauce among 4 warm plates and arrange 2 chops on each. Sprinkle with parsley and serve.

STEAK WITH SHALLOT SAUCE

—

YIELD: 4 SERVINGS

A black cast-iron skillet is one of the most important items in my kitchen. It is heavy, retains high heat, and never wears out. If it is properly seasoned and cleaned, food will never stick. It is perfect for cooking steak over very high heat and requires very little cooking fat. When the oil comes to a smoking point, add the steak and sear it. Remember to remove the steak from the refrigerator ahead of time so it is not cold when you place it in the skillet.

4 boneless shell steaks (about 6 ounces each), with fat removed
Salt and freshly ground pepper, to taste
1 teaspoon olive oil
½ cup thinly sliced shallots
¼ cup dry red wine
1 tablespoon butter
2 tablespoons finely chopped parsley

1. Sprinkle the steaks on both sides with salt and pepper.

2. Heat a cast-iron skillet or heavy bottomed frying pan large enough to hold the steaks in one layer until it is very hot. Add the oil and quickly coat the bottom of the skillet. Add the steaks and cook until well browned, about 3 minutes on each side for rare. For medium rare, cook 4-5 minutes on each side. Transfer to a warm platter.

3. Pour off all the fat from the skillet. Add the shallots and cook, stirring often, until they are golden brown, 2-3 minutes. Add the wine, cook briefly, and add any juices that have accumulated around the steaks. Cook a few minutes longer, then stir in the butter.

4. Place the steaks on individual plates, pour the shallot sauce over, and sprinkle with parsley.

LIGHT MEATBALLS WITH YOGURT SAUCE

YIELD: 4 SERVINGS

These meatballs are lower in fat because I use ground turkey or chicken instead of a pork, veal, and beef combination. And in the sauce, I substitute yogurt for heavy cream. Serve these meatballs with noodles or rice.

2 tablespoons olive oil
½ cup finely chopped onion
1 pound lean ground turkey or chicken, or a blend of the two
½ cup fresh bread crumbs
½ cup low-fat (2%) milk
1 large egg
Salt and freshly ground pepper, to taste
Freshly grated nutmeg
⅛ teaspoon ground allspice
1 tablespoon all-purpose flour
1 cup fresh or canned chicken broth
1 cup plain low-fat yogurt, drained
1 tablespoon finely chopped fresh dill

1. Melt 1 tablespoon of the olive oil in a small skillet, then add the onion. Cook, stirring, over low heat until wilted. Let cool.

2. In a large mixing bowl, combine the turkey or chicken, onion, bread crumbs, milk, egg, salt, pepper, nutmeg, and allspice. Blend well with your hands.

3. Shape the mixture into 28 or more meatballs, each 1-1½ inches in diameter.

4. Heat the remaining tablespoon olive oil over medium-high heat in a large nonstick skillet. Add the meatballs several at a time, and cook, turning carefully with a spatula so they brown evenly, for about 10 minutes. When done, transfer to a warm platter.

5. Pour off most of the fat from the skillet and add the flour. Blend well with a wire whisk, then add the chicken broth. Bring to a boil, stirring, and cook for about 1 minute. Add the yogurt and cook for 1 minute more. Check for seasoning, then return the meatballs to the skillet. Bring to a simmer to reheat. Transfer to a serving platter, sprinkle with dill, and serve.

BOW TIE PASTA WITH GOAT CHEESE

YIELD: 4 SERVINGS

Goat's milk contains less fat than cow's milk or sheep's milk, and soft cheeses usually contain less fat than hard cheeses. Adding the goat cheese at the end of this recipe helps to bind all the ingredients and thicken the sauce.

1 pound green beans
6 ounces soft goat cheese of your choice
¾ pound bow tie pasta
2 tablespoons olive oil
1 tablespoon chopped garlic
4 large ripe plum tomatoes, seeded and diced
1 small red bell pepper, cored, seeded, and cut into small cubes
1 jalapeño pepper, seeded and finely chopped
Salt and freshly ground pepper, to taste
¼ cup coarsely chopped fresh basil

1. Trim off and discard the ends of the beans, then cut them into 1½-inch lengths.

2. Crumble the goat cheese and let come to room temperature.

3. In a large pot, bring 4 cups salted water to a boil. Add the beans and pasta. Bring to a boil again and cook 6-8 minutes, stirring. Test for doneness; do not overcook. The pasta and the beans should be al dente. Drain and reserve ¼ cup of the cooking liquid.

4. Meanwhile, in a large saucepan, heat 1 tablespoon of the olive oil, add the garlic, and cook briefly, without letting it brown. Add the tomatoes, red pepper, jalapeño pepper, salt, and pepper. Cook over medium heat, stirring, about 5 minutes.

5. Add the pasta and the beans, along with the reserved cooking liquid, goat cheese, remaining tablespoon olive oil, and basil. Toss well, adjust the seasoning, and cook briefly until thick. Serve immediately.

SUGAR SNAP PEAS WITH CARROTS

YIELD: 4 SERVINGS

I love to eat sugar snap peas. If fresh, they are always tender. They should be bright green, unblemished, and not at all dried out.

½ pound sugar snap peas
4 medium carrots (about ½ pound)
1 tablespoon butter
1 teaspoon finely chopped fresh mint
¼ teaspoon ground cumin
Salt and freshly ground pepper, to taste

1. Trim and discard the tips of the peas; remove strings.

2. Scrape and trim the carrots, then cut them into slices about ⅛ inch thick.

3. In a medium saucepan, bring enough salted water to cover the vegetables to a boil. Add the carrots and cook for about 3 minutes. Add the peas and cook for another 3 minutes or until tender-crisp. Drain immediately.

4. Return the peas and carrots to the saucepan and add the butter, mint, cumin, and salt and pepper. Stir and blend well. Serve immediately.

NEW BITTERSWEET CHOCOLATE SORBET

YIELD: 10 SERVINGS

As an alternative to Roger's Chocolate Beignets, here is a sorbet made with two kinds of chocolate. The egg white adds an airiness to the consistency.

½ pound bittersweet or semisweet chocolate
3 ounces sweet chocolate, grated
¾ cup sugar
1 large egg white, slightly beaten

1. Melt the bittersweet chocolate slowly in the top of a double boiler.

2. Blend 3 cups lukewarm water with the melted chocolate. Add the grated sweet chocolate and the sugar and blend well.

3. Pour the mixture into an ice-cream freezer and follow the manufacturer's instructions. When the mixture begins to freeze, add the egg white and resume freezing.

OPPOSITE: *Pieces from Roger Souvereyns's collection of antique spoons, upon which appetizers are artfully arranged for service.*

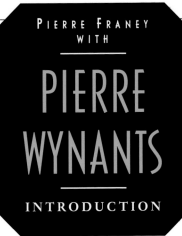

The meeting of old and new comes to mind when dining at Comme Chez Soi, the finest restaurant in Brussels. Indeed, at the top of the restaurant's menu is the inscription, *"Depuis 1929, quatre générations de traditions et d'évolution"* ("Since 1929, four generations of tradition and evolution"). Pierre Wynants and his family have been running the restaurant for more than fifty years. Their menu is a combination of classic Belgian cuisine, with its rich sauces of butter and eggs, and a more modern, lighter approach to food.

Started by his grandfather as a modest bistro serving traditional Belgian food, the restaurant has evolved into an establishment of the highest quality, with a three-star rating from the *Guide Michelin*. Pierre has great respect for tradition, having been trained as a young man by his father, Louis, in the restaurant's kitchen and then having apprenticed in two great restaurants in Paris, Le Grand Véfour and La Tour d'Argent. To learn English, he also spent time in a

Opposite: The dining room is characterized by Art Nouveau details and stained glass skylights. Right: Pierre Franey and Pierre Wynants in the Comme Chez Soi kitchen.

ABOVE: *A dramatic floral arrangement fills the bay window of the Comme Chez Soi dining room.* OPPOSITE: *Comme Chez Soi's classic menu.* OVERLEAF: *The restaurant's front entrance, not far from the Brussels city center.*

London hotel. Although Pierre enjoyed his stays abroad, he longed to return home. Working in the kitchen with his father, Pierre soon earned a reputation as a young and innovative chef. He is a perfectionist and demands of his staff the highest standards in preparing and presenting the restaurant's cuisine.

Pierre is proud of his city and took me on a personal tour, showing off his favorite eating places—a brasserie where we ate the classic Belgian dish *moules et frites* (mussels and French fries) served with Belgian beer; a corner stand serving the lightest of thick Belgian waffles; the best chocolate shop in town; and, of course, a walk through the Grande Place, Brussels' medieval square in the heart of the city. We also went to watch his favorite local soccer team play in a match.

But my favorite place to visit was Pierre's restaurant, Comme Chez Soi. It is located on a quiet square not far from the center of Brussels. Small and intimate with an Art Nouveau decor, the restaurant has dark, polished wood paneling, stained glass windows, oil paintings of landscapes, and bowls of fresh flowers that make for an inviting setting. Pierre's wife, Marie-Thérèse, and their daughter Laurence are in charge of the dining room. They are warm and friendly and make sure that their guests are treated with the greatest care. Pierre is in the kitchen working with his son-in-law, Lionel, and a young and talented kitchen crew. The wall in the back of the kitchen is covered with white tiles that carry the signatures of hundreds of famous people who have eaten at Comme Chez Soi—artists, politicians, chefs, movie stars, people from all walks of life. I was truly honored when Pierre asked me to sign my own tile.

The restaurant's menu pays homage to Belgian cuisine, serving classic dishes such as asparagus Flemish style and fillets of sole with a rich mousselike sauce made with a

white wine from Luxembourg, mushrooms, and small shrimp. The sauces for both dishes are made with butter and eggs. Low-fat and low-calorie they are not—but they are quite delicious. On the other hand, Pierre also likes to cook with olive oil instead of butter, and he creates sauces that are light in style. For example, he cooked a dish for me that he created that very day—a chicken sautéed in a little olive oil and served with small, delicate snails, a specialty of Belgium (see page 159). This dish is an example of how he has adapted his cooking to suit the needs of a clientele seeking a cuisine that is not too rich but that retains the flavors of classic Belgian dishes.

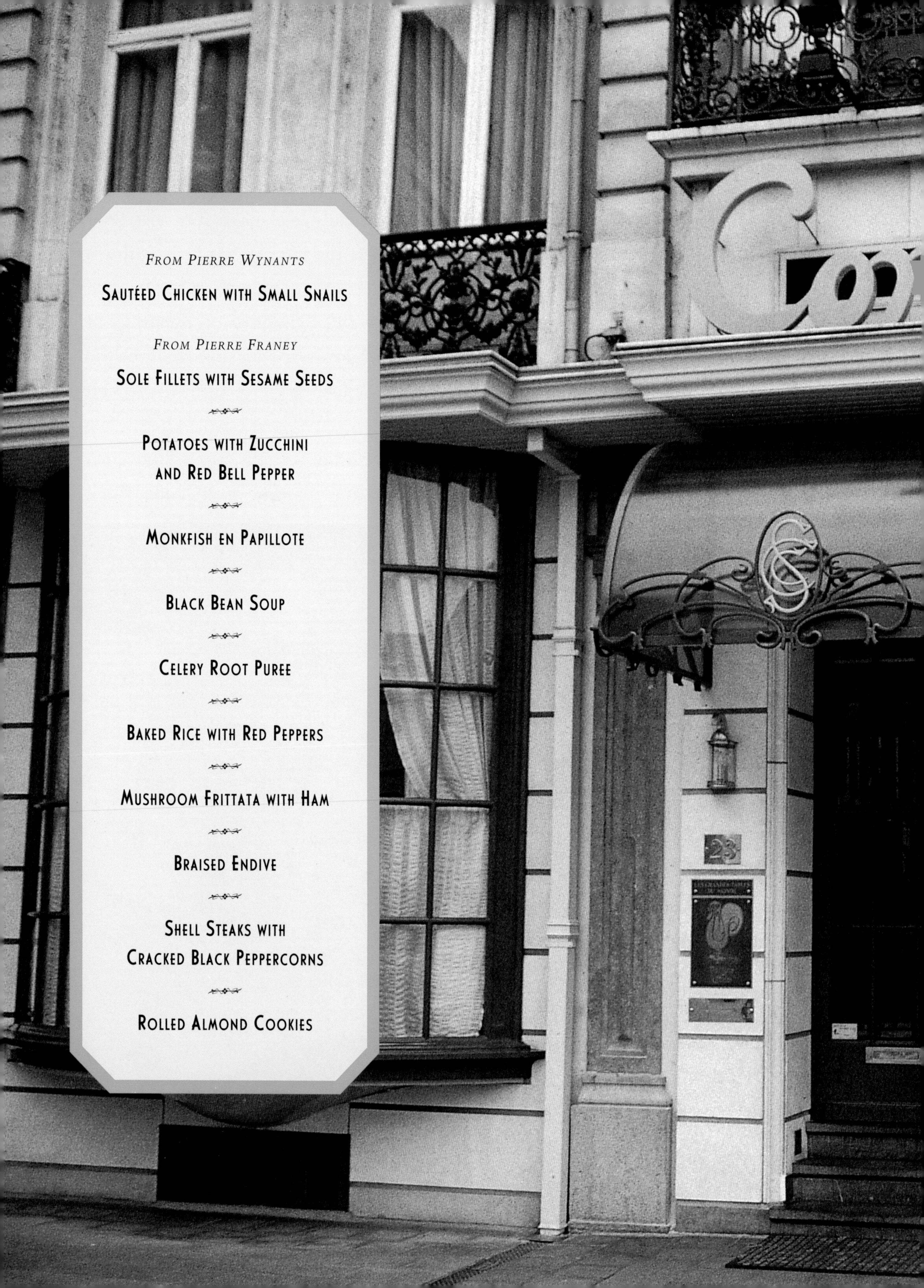

FROM PIERRE WYNANTS

SAUTÉED CHICKEN WITH SMALL SNAILS

FROM PIERRE FRANEY

SOLE FILLETS WITH SESAME SEEDS

❧

**POTATOES WITH ZUCCHINI
AND RED BELL PEPPER**

❧

MONKFISH EN PAPILLOTE

❧

BLACK BEAN SOUP

❧

CELERY ROOT PUREE

❧

BAKED RICE WITH RED PEPPERS

❧

MUSHROOM FRITTATA WITH HAM

❧

BRAISED ENDIVE

❧

**SHELL STEAKS WITH
CRACKED BLACK PEPPERCORNS**

❧

ROLLED ALMOND COOKIES

SAUTÉED CHICKEN WITH SMALL SNAILS

YIELD: 4 SERVINGS

Pierre Wynants prepared this recipe with special small land snails found in Belgium, petits gris de Namur, which are no more than a quarter inch in diameter. They are unavailable in the United States, so I recommend using imported canned snails from France.

The free-range chicken came from a nearby chicken farm and was very lean and tender; you can find free-range chickens in many U.S. supermarkets today. Accompany this dish with rice or potatoes.

1 3½-pound free-range chicken

2 tablespoons olive oil

¼ pound large white mushrooms, cleaned and quartered

12 small white pearl onions, peeled

18 canned snails imported from France, drained with juices reserved

8 scallions, cleaned and trimmed with most of the green part removed, quartered lengthwise and finely chopped

Salt and freshly ground pepper, to taste

1 cup fresh or canned chicken broth

1 cup fresh coarsely chopped parsley

1 tablespoon lemon juice

1. Remove the legs of the chicken and separate the thighs and drumsticks with a sharp knife. Reserve the drumsticks for other use. Bone the thighs. Cut each thigh into 4 equal pieces. Remove the breast meat from the chicken carcass and cut each breast half into 2 equal pieces. Next, remove the wings. Cut off the wing tips and discard or use for chicken broth. Cut each wing at the joint into 2 pieces. You should end up with 16 chicken pieces.

2. In a heavy cast-iron Dutch oven large enough to accommodate the chicken pieces in one layer, heat the olive oil over high heat. Add the mushrooms, pearl onions, snails, and scallions. Add salt and pepper and cook quickly, stirring constantly, until lightly browned, about 3 minutes. Remove contents with a slotted spoon. Set aside, leaving the oil in the pot.

3. Add the chicken pieces skin side down. Season with salt and pepper, and cook until lightly browned, turning often. Drain off excess fat, then add the broth and snail juice. Bring to a boil, reduce the heat, and simmer until reduced by one-third.

4. Return the mushroom mixture to the pot, along with the parsley and lemon juice. Bring to a simmer and cook for 3-4 minutes. Check for seasoning, then serve immediately on 4 warm plates.

SOLE FILLETS WITH SESAME SEEDS

YIELD: 4 SERVINGS

This is a quick low-fat recipe. Instead of dipping the fillets in whole eggs, I use egg whites to cut down on the fat. The sesame seeds give a nice toasted flavor to the fish; be careful not to burn them.

2 large egg whites

Dash of Tabasco sauce

Salt and freshly ground white pepper, to taste

1 cup sesame seeds

8 skinless fillets of sole, fluke, or flounder (about 3 ounces each)

3 tablespoons olive oil

Potatoes with Zucchini and Red Bell Pepper (see page 162)

4 sprigs parsley, for garnish

4 lemon wedges

1. Beat the egg whites briefly with a wire whisk, adding 2 tablespoons water, the Tabasco, and salt and pepper.

2. Place the sesame seeds in a large, flat dish. Dip the fillets one at a time in the egg mixture to coat well. Remove any excess, then pat both sides of the fillets with sesame seeds, making certain the seeds adhere.

3. Heat the oil in a large nonstick skillet over medium-high heat. Add enough fillets to make one layer without overlapping. Cook until golden brown on one side, 1½-2 minutes. Turn and cook about 1½ minutes on the second side. The cooking time will depend on the thickness of the fish. As the fillets are cooked, transfer them to a warm platter. Continue cooking until the fillets are done.

4. To serve, place 2 fillets on each of 4 warm plates. Arrange the vegetables attractively next to the fillets. Add a parsley sprig and a lemon wedge to each plate and serve immediately.

POTATOES WITH ZUCCHINI AND RED BELL PEPPER

YIELD: 4 SERVINGS

Serve this side dish with fish, meat, or chicken. You may prepare and steam the potatoes and zucchini in advance, then sauté them with the remaining ingredients just before serving.

8 small red-skinned potatoes (about ¾ pound), peeled and cut in half

2-3 small zucchini (about ¾ pound), trimmed and cut in half lengthwise, then into 1½-inch strips

2 tablespoons olive oil

1 red bell pepper, cored, seeded, and cut into 1½-inch strips

1 tablespoon finely chopped shallots

Salt and freshly ground pepper, to taste

3 tablespoons fresh lemon juice

3 tablespoons chopped fresh coriander (cilantro) or parsley

1. Place the potatoes on the rack of a steamer over boiling water and steam for 10 minutes. Add the zucchini and cook for 3 minutes more. Do not overcook. Drain, reserving ¼ cup of the cooking liquid.

2. Heat the oil in a large nonstick skillet. Add the red pepper strips and cook until wilted. Add the potatoes, zucchini, shallots, salt, and pepper and cook, stirring, for about 1 minute. Add the cooking liquid, then cook for a few more minutes until the liquid is mostly reduced. Add the lemon juice and coriander. Toss over medium heat for about 30 seconds and serve.

MONKFISH EN PAPILLOTE

YIELD: 4 SERVINGS

This recipe can be prepared in advance and placed in the refrigerator. Remove it 30 minutes before cooking and place in a preheated oven just before serving. I prefer using parchment paper rather than aluminum foil because it is more attractive to serve, although the aluminum foil is easier to use. It is important that the papillotes be well sealed, otherwise they will not puff.

½ cup julienned carrots, in 1-inch lengths
½ cup julienned fennel, in 1-inch lengths
½ cup julienned celery, in 1-inch lengths
½ cup julienned red bell pepper, in 1-inch lengths
½ cup coarsely chopped scallions
½ cup dry white wine
Salt and freshly ground pepper, to taste
2 tablespoons olive oil
4 skinless monkfish fillets (about 4 ounces each), trimmed
Dash of Tabasco sauce
3 tablespoons chopped fresh dill

1. Preheat the oven to 475° F.

2. Spread a large sheet of aluminum foil or parchment paper on a flat surface. Invert a 12-inch round cake pan, plate, or lid on the foil. Trace around the pan with a sharp knife to make a 12-inch circle. Repeat 3 more times.

3. In a medium saucepan, combine the vegetables and wine. Bring to a boil, then add the salt and pepper. Cover and cook until the wine is reduced by half, taking care not to overcook the vegetables. Remove from the heat and set aside to cool.

4. Place the foil or paper rounds on a flat surface and brush lightly with 2 teaspoons olive oil. On each round, slightly below the center, place a monkfish fillet and sprinkle with salt and pepper.

5. Divide the cooked vegetables and their liquid into 4 equal portions and place a portion over each fish fillet. Drizzle 1 teaspoon olive oil over the vegetables in each papillote, and add a dash of Tabasco to each serving. Spread the chopped dill over all.

6. Fold the top half of the foil or paper over to enclose the contents completely while leaving some room for expansion. Make narrow overlapping folds over the edges and crimp as tightly as possible to seal. Arrange the packages on a baking dish. (At this point you can place in the refrigerator until ready to cook.) Bake for 15 minutes.

7. To serve, remove the papillotes with a flat spatula, taking care not to tear the foil or paper.

BLACK BEAN SOUP

YIELD: 10-12 SERVINGS

Black beans are a good source of protein and are low in fat. This is a good winter soup and is excellent when reheated. You may have to add some chicken broth or water to make it less thick. Sometimes I like to add ¼ cup dry sherry or Madeira wine.

1 pound dried black beans

2 tablespoons olive oil

¼ pound raw cured ham, such as lean Smithfield or country ham, cut into ½-inch cubes

4 cups chopped onion

¼ cup finely minced garlic

3½ quarts fresh or canned chicken broth

Salt and freshly ground pepper, to taste

½ teaspoon cayenne pepper

2 tablespoons red wine vinegar

¼ cup dry sherry

¼ cup drained plain low-fat yogurt

¼ cup chopped fresh coriander (cilantro)

Thin slices of lime, with peel on

1. Rinse the beans well and pick them over to remove foreign particles, if any. Place the beans in a medium mixing bowl, add cold water to cover by about 4 inches, and let stand overnight. Or place in a large pot, bring to a boil, and cook for 1 minute, then cover and let stand for 1 hour.

2. Heat the oil in a casserole or Dutch oven over medium-high heat and add the ham, 3½ cups of the onions, and the garlic. Cook, stirring, about 5 minutes or until wilted. Drain the beans well and add them to the pot. Add the broth and bring to a boil. Add the salt, pepper, and cayenne. Reduce the heat to low, partially cover, and cook, stirring occasionally, for 3-4 hours or until beans are tender.

3. Put half the soup with the beans through a food mill or sieve or puree in a blender. Return this mixture to the pot and stir to blend. Add the vinegar and sherry and check for seasoning. Serve piping hot in soup bowls with a spoonful of yogurt in the middle, sprinkle coriander on top, and place the remaining ½ cup chopped onion and the lime slices on the side for those who desire them.

CELERY ROOT PUREE

YIELD: 4 SERVINGS

Celery root—a variety of celery with a delicious bulbous root—is beginning to catch on in the United States. It blends particularly well with potatoes, as in this recipe.

2 celery root (also called knob celery or celeriac),
    about 1½ pounds
½ pound potatoes
Salt, to taste
1 tablespoon olive oil
1 cup hot low-fat milk
Dash of freshly ground nutmeg
Pinch of cayenne pepper

1. Peel the celery root and cut into 1-inch cubes. Peel the potatoes and cut them into 2½-inch cubes.

2. Place the celery root and potatoes in a large pot with water to cover and add salt. Bring to a boil and cook until tender, about 15 minutes. Drain well.

3. Put the celery root and potatoes through a food mill or mash with a potato masher. Do not use a food processor or blender. Add the olive oil and blend with a spatula. Add the hot milk a little at a time, and blend well. Add nutmeg, salt, and cayenne and blend again. Check for seasoning.

BAKED RICE WITH RED PEPPERS

YIELD: 4 SERVINGS

I prefer to use converted (parboiled) rice. After cooking, the grains remain slightly firm, retain their shape, and do not stick together or become gluey.

1 tablespoon olive oil
2 tablespoons minced onion
1 red bell pepper, cored, seeded, and cut into ½-inch cubes
¼ teaspoon minced garlic
1 cup converted rice
1½ cups fresh or canned chicken broth or water
2 sprigs parsley
1 sprig thyme, or ¼ teaspoon dried
½ bay leaf
⅛ teaspoon cayenne pepper or Tabasco sauce, to taste

1. Preheat the oven to 400° F.

2. Heat the oil in a large, heavy ovenproof saucepan and cook the onion, red pepper, and garlic, stirring with a wooden spoon until the onion is translucent. Add the rice and stir briefly over low heat until all the grains are coated with oil.

3. Stir in the broth, making sure there are no lumps in the rice. Add the parsley, thyme, bay leaf, and cayenne. Cover with a close-fitting lid and place in the oven.

4. Bake the rice exactly 17 minutes. Remove the cover and discard the bay leaf, parsley, and thyme sprigs. Stir with a 2-pronged fork and serve.

MUSHROOM FRITTATA WITH HAM

YIELD: 4 SERVINGS

My wife, Betty, and I love this dish. We eat it warm in the winter and cold in the summer. It can be made in advance and with any other kind of vegetable, such as spinach, diced tomatoes and zucchini, or cubed eggplant. Cornichons (sour gherkins) and a tossed salad go well with this dish.

1 pound small red-skinned potatoes
2 tablespoons olive oil
½ pound mushrooms, thinly sliced
1 cup thinly sliced small white onion
1 red bell pepper, cored, seeded, and cut into thin strips
1 cup diced cooked lean ham
1 tablespoon minced garlic
Salt and freshly ground pepper, to taste
8 large eggs, at room temperature
½ cup fresh basil or flat-leaf parsley

1. Place the potatoes in a medium saucepan and add water to cover and a pinch of salt. Bring to a boil and cook, simmering, until tender, about 20 minutes. Drain. When the potatoes are cooled enough to handle, peel and slice them ¼ inch thick. Set aside.

2. Heat 1 tablespoon of the oil in a large nonstick skillet. Add the potatoes and cook gently, stirring often, until they are golden brown, 5-6 minutes. Remove and set aside.

3. Leave the oil in the pan and return the pan to high heat. Add the mushrooms and cook, stirring often, until they start to turn brown. Add the onion, red pepper strips, ham, garlic, salt, and pepper. Cook, stirring and shaking the pan, for 5 minutes.

4. Meanwhile, break the eggs into a mixing bowl, add salt and pepper, and beat well with a fork. In the same skillet, add the remaining tablespoon of oil over medium-high heat. Add the potatoes, mushroom mixture, and basil and cook, stirring, over high heat for 2 minutes.

5. Beat the egg mixture again and pour it over the potato-mushroom mixture. Cook, stirring from the bottom with a wooden spatula, until the eggs start to set, about 2 minutes. Cover and cook over medium heat for about 3 minutes or until done.

6. Place a large, round serving dish over the skillet and quickly invert both the skillet and the dish, letting the frittata fall into the dish. It should be golden brown on top. Serve immediately.

BRAISED ENDIVE

—

YIELD: 4 SERVINGS

In Belgium and elsewhere, endive are cultivated in two ways. The traditional method is to plant the roots under cover, with no light, and to harvest the shoots in winter and spring only. In the new method, the endive roots are stored in the dark at a very cold temperature. As endive are needed, the roots are removed to special trays and the shoots are grown in temperature-controlled circulating water. This way, endive are available throughout the year.

8 medium unblemished Belgian endive
Salt and freshly ground white pepper, to taste
¼ teaspoon ground cumin
1 tablespoon fresh lemon juice
1 tablespoon olive oil
2 tablespoons finely chopped fresh chervil or parsley

1. Wash the endive and trim the stems.

2. Place the endive in a heavy nonreactive skillet large enough to hold them in one layer. Sprinkle the endive with salt and pepper, cumin, and lemon juice. Add ½ cup water and the olive oil and cover tightly. Bring to a boil, then simmer about 25 minutes or until the water is evaporated. Uncover the endive and brown lightly on both sides. Sprinkle with chervil or parsley and serve.

Endive are trimmed by workers at a nearby farm before they are packed for delivery to the market.

SHELL STEAKS WITH CRACKED BLACK PEPPERCORNS

YIELD: 4 SERVINGS

You can also prepare a boneless rib steak using this recipe. Ask your butcher to cut it from the eye of the rib because there is less fat in the meat.

4 boneless shell steaks (about 6 ounces each), with the fat removed

Salt, to taste

¼ cup black peppercorns

1 tablespoon olive oil

1 tablespoon finely chopped shallots

2 tablespoons finely chopped onion

½ cup Cabernet or other dry red wine

½ cup fresh or canned chicken broth

2 teaspoons tomato paste

1 tablespoon Dijon mustard

1 tablespoon unsalted butter

2 tablespoons finely chopped parsley

1. Sprinkle the steaks with salt.

2. Using a mallet or the bottom of a heavy saucepan, crush the peppercorns, taking care that they are not made too fine. Sprinkle them evenly over the steaks on both sides. Press down with your hands to help the peppercorns adhere to the meat.

3. Heat the oil in a heavy cast-iron skillet large enough to hold the steaks in one layer. When the skillet is hot and almost smoking, add the steaks. Cook over medium-high heat about 3 minutes or until browned, then turn. Cook for 2-3 minutes more for medium rare, depending on the thickness of the steaks. Remove to a warm platter.

4. Pour the fat from the skillet and add the shallots and onion. Cook, stirring, until they are wilted; do not brown. Add the wine and reduce by half. Add the broth, tomato paste, and mustard. Blend well, and cook for a few minutes until smooth. There should be about ½ cup. Add any liquid that may have accumulated around the steaks, and bring to a simmer. Remove skillet from the heat and swirl in the butter. Check for seasoning.

5. To serve, pour the sauce over the steaks and sprinkle with parsley.

ROLLED ALMOND COOKIES

YIELD: ABOUT 32 COOKIES

These cookies are very popular in European restaurants. They are very thin and crispy and become nearly transparent or lacelike when baked. Serve them with a sorbet, or as an accompaniment to coffee at the end of a meal.

1 cup slivered almonds
½ cup superfine sugar
3 tablespoons all-purpose flour
1 large egg
1 teaspoon vanilla extract

1. Preheat the oven to 350° F.

2. Place the almonds in a medium bowl and add the sugar, flour, egg, and vanilla. Blend well and leave the batter in the refrigerator for 1½ hours before baking.

3. On a buttered or parchment-paper–lined baking sheet, drop the cookies by tablespoonfuls, with about 3 inches in between. Flatten each mound with a fork dipped in milk. The cookies have to be nearly flat; if not, the center of the cookie will not bake. Place 16-18 cookies on a baking sheet and bake the sheets one at a time in the center of the oven for 10 minutes, or until the cookies are golden brown.

4. As soon as the cookies are baked, remove them from the oven. While still hot, lift each cookie off the baking sheet with a spatula and roll it around a rolling pin to shape it. Allow to cool. These cookies can be kept for 6 days in a tightly sealed container.

The kitchen of Comme Chez Soi is seen through the dining room window, framed here by the skylights and the highly polished, dark wood moldings.

PIERRE FRANEY
WITH

MAARTJE BOUDELING

INTRODUCTION

The quiet charm of the province of Zeeland, in the southwestern corner of the Netherlands, is just the right setting for Inter Scaldes, the manor house and two-star seafood restaurant of Maartje and Kees Boudeling. This is the land of "polders," low-lying areas that have been reclaimed from the North Sea and protected by dikes. Windmills and modern pumps help to keep the sea away, creating a rich land filled with orchards and farms. Fishing is plentiful, and the local fishermen bring in daily catches of lobster, mussels, oysters, turbot, and a variety of other fish.

Nestled on the narrowest part of Beveland, a peninsula jutting out into the North Sea, Inter Scaldes has an international reputation for its excellent preparation of seafood. Maartje, who is the chef de cuisine, grew up in nearby Yerseke, a small fishing village where her father was an oysterman. She spent time in France, training with chefs in the very best restaurants. Her husband, Kees, comes from a local family that has been in the hotel business for more than one hundred years. Their combined skills make for a husband-and-wife team that thoughtfully caters to their clients' needs, in both the restaurant and the hotel. They carefully designed Inter Scaldes in the style of an English country manor house, with a thatched roof and a walled-in English garden in the backyard. Graceful statues decorate the garden. The hotel-

Inter Scaldes, Maartje and Kees Boudeling's seafood restaurant in the Netherlands.

restaurant sits alone in the middle of farmland, with apple and pear orchards nearby. The restaurant is airy and open with a light green decor, hanging plants, and white rattan furniture. There is an extensive wine cellar stocked with an impressive number of French wines.

The sea serves as an inspiration for Maartje's cooking. Her preparation is simple and light because, like all top chefs, she believes that the freshness of ingredients is the key to a good cuisine. Her menu is seasonal and changes depending on what fish and local produce are available. Sea asters—greens that grow in the marshes in the springtime—are used in her seafood salads or cooked and served as an accompaniment to other dishes. I visited in the late spring, when asparagus was in season.

Maartje and Kees brought me to a nearby farm, one of their suppliers, where white asparagus was being harvested. Later that day we went out on a lobster boat to watch the fishermen haul in the day's catch. Not surprisingly, the restaurant's menu that evening included a lobster salad with white asparagus in a truffle vinaigrette, made with the very ingredients I had seen harvested that day. The salad was light and so fresh!

LEFT: *Pierre samples the local herring.*
ABOVE: *Maartje Boudeling and Pierre examine a lobster from the day's catch.* OPPOSITE: *Each place setting at Inter Scaldes is punctuated with a crisply folded napkin.* OVERLEAF: *The restaurant's airy, light-filled dining room.*

The next day Maartje invited me into her kitchen. She prepared Warm Oysters Vinaigrette (see page 178), one of her specialties. She cuts down on the oil in the vinaigrette by using the juice from the oysters, which gives the vinaigrette a slight hint of the sea. She also prepared a Scallop and Shrimp Salad (see page 176) in which the scallops were basted in a basil marinade. Both recipes require very fresh seafood and use fresh vegetables and herbs for flavoring.

SCALLOP AND SHRIMP SALAD

—

YIELD: 4 SERVINGS

This recipe calls for tiny cooked and shelled European shrimp, but tiny Maine shrimp can be substituted. If not available, use other small shrimp. It is important that the scallops be very fresh, because they are not cooked and are placed in the marinade only briefly.

FOR THE MARINADE:

¼ cup extra-virgin olive oil
½ cup basil leaves, loosely packed
2 tablespoons lemon juice
Salt and freshly ground pepper, to taste

FOR THE VINAIGRETTE:

1 tablespoon Dijon mustard
1 tablespoon aged red wine vinegar
¼ cup extra-virgin olive oil
Salt and freshly ground pepper, to taste
16 large, very fresh sea scallops, cut crosswise into 4 even
    slices
4 cups small, tender mixed salad greens, such as mesclun and
    mâche
3 cups coarsely chopped mixed herbs, such as parsley, dill,
    tarragon, chervil, and a few mint leaves
1 pound small shrimp, cooked and peeled

1. Make the marinade: Heat the oil to lukewarm in a small saucepan, add the basil, remove from heat, and let stand 1 hour. Strain. Add the lemon juice, salt, and pepper. Blend well.

2. Make the vinaigrette: In a large bowl, combine the mustard and vinegar and blend well with a wire whisk. Slowly whisk in the olive oil and season with salt and pepper. Set aside.

3. Place the scallop slices in a large bowl and add the marinade. Toss well, making sure they are well coated. Let stand 15 minutes.

4. Just before serving, add the salad greens and fresh herbs to the vinaigrette. Toss well.

5. To serve, divide the salad greens among 4 large serving plates by piling up the greens in the center of each plate. Place 16 scallops in overlapping slices in a circle around each mound. Place the shrimp around the edges in small mounds, dividing them equally among the 4 plates, and pour the leftover marinade over.

NOTE: If you need to cook the shrimp, here's an easy way to do it: Put the shrimp in a pot of water with a little thyme, a bay leaf, a few parsley sprigs, a dash of Tabasco sauce, salt, and a few peppercorns. Bring to a simmer and turn off the heat. Let stand for 5 minutes. Drain and peel when they have cooled down.

WARM OYSTERS VINAIGRETTE

—

YIELD: 4 SERVINGS

It is important that the oysters be opened at the last minute so they are very fresh when you are ready to cook and so you can retain their juices. Maartje uses aged red wine vinegar, which is smoother in taste and less sharp than regular vinegar. It is available in specialty food shops in the United States, but can be expensive.

24 Belon, bluepoint, Eastern, or Malpeque oysters, shucked, with ¼ cup juice and bottom shells reserved

2 teaspoons aged red wine vinegar

2 tablespoons olive oil

Sea salt, for garnish (see Note)

1 pound seaweed, blanched slightly, cooled, and drained (optional)

¼ cup cored, seeded, and finely diced red bell pepper

2 tablespoons chopped chives

1. Preheat the oven to 350° F.

2. In a small saucepan, combine the reserved oyster juice, vinegar, and oil. Blend well with a wire whisk and heat slightly, just to lukewarm.

3. Place the oyster shells in the oven to warm them.

4. Place the shucked oysters and any remaining juice in a medium saucepan over low heat to warm the oysters. They should be just warmed; the edges will start to bubble. Do not allow them to boil. Remove from heat.

5. Place a small amount of sea salt in the centers of 4 plates to form a little mound. Arrange the seaweed around the salt to serve as a base for the oysters. Place 6 warmed shells on top of the seaweed and a warm oyster on each shell. Add the red pepper to the vinaigrette and spoon over each oyster. Sprinkle with chives and serve immediately.

NOTE: If sea salt is not available, kosher salt may be used.

SAUTÉED SWEET PEPPERS AND ZUCCHINI

—

YIELD: 4 SERVINGS

This recipe can be served in a number of ways: as a cold appetizer, as a relish to accompany cold cuts, or as a warm side dish.

2 cups thinly sliced zucchini, in ¼-inch pieces

1 small yellow bell pepper, cored, seeded, and cut into thin strips

1 small red bell pepper, cored, seeded, and cut into thin strips

1 tablespoon olive oil

2 tablespoons finely chopped shallots

1 tablespoon finely chopped fresh rosemary, or 1 teaspoon dried

⅛ teaspoon hot red pepper flakes

Salt and freshly ground pepper, to taste

2 tablespoons finely chopped chives

1. Place the zucchini and bell pepper in a steamer over boiling water and steam until just tender, about 2 minutes. Do not overcook.

2. Heat the olive oil in a large nonstick skillet. Add the shallots and cook briefly over medium-hot heat until wilted. Add the zucchini mixture, rosemary, red pepper flakes, and salt and pepper. Sauté lightly, being careful not to overcook. Sprinkle with chives and serve immediately.

RED MULLET WITH TOMATOES

—

YIELD: 4 SERVINGS

I like to cook fish fillets with the skin on. It helps to keep the fish together and retains moistness. It is important not to overcook fish. You can test for doneness by putting the tip of a knife into the flesh and seeing if it is cooked in the center. Let the cooked fish rest a few minutes before serving to make sure the heat has been evenly dispersed. Serve this with Sautéed Sweet Peppers and Zucchini (see page 179).

8 skin-on and scaled red mullet fillets (3 ounces each); or use red snapper, sea bass, or flounder

Salt and freshly ground pepper, to taste

⅓ cup low-fat (1%) milk

⅓ cup all-purpose flour, for dusting

3 tablespoons olive oil

2 cups seeded and diced ripe plum tomatoes, in ¼-inch cubes

1 tablespoon finely chopped garlic

2 tablespoons lemon juice

4 tablespoons finely chopped parsley

1. Season the fillets with salt and pepper. Dip each fillet in milk and drain. Dredge in the flour, making sure it adheres, and remove the excess flour.

2. Heat 2 tablespoons of the oil in a heavy nonstick skillet large enough to hold the fish in one layer. Add the fish fillets skin side up and sauté over high heat until lightly browned, about 3 minutes. Rotate the fillets in the pan so they brown evenly. Turn over onto the skin side and continue cooking briefly until done. The total cooking time will depend on the thickness of the fillets; do not overcook. Remove and keep warm.

3. Add the tomatoes, salt, and pepper to the skillet. Cook until the tomatoes are soft, then add the garlic, remaining tablespoon olive oil, and the lemon juice. Cook briefly; do not brown the garlic.

4. To serve, divide the tomato sauce among 4 warm serving plates. Remove the skin from the fillets and place the fillets over the sauce. Sprinkle with parsley before serving.

VEAL SCALOPPINE WITH MUSTARD

—

YIELD: 4 SERVINGS

To ensure tenderness, veal scaloppine should be cut against the grain from a single muscle. This will also prevent the veal pieces from buckling during cooking. A good butcher will cut it this way.

8 thin slices veal scaloppine, cut from the loin or top round (about 1¼ pounds)

Salt and freshly ground pepper, to taste

1 tablespoon Dijon mustard

1 tablespoon mustard seeds

2 tablespoons olive oil

2 tablespoons chopped fresh herbs, such as tarragon, basil, chervil, parsley

1½ cups fresh tomato sauce (see page 185)

1. Place the veal between sheets of plastic wrap and pound evenly with a flat mallet or meat pounder until very thin. Remove the plastic and sprinkle on both sides with salt and pepper.

2. With a pastry brush, spread half the mustard on one side of the scaloppine. Sprinkle half the mustard seeds over, turn the scaloppine, and spread the remaining mustard over them. Sprinkle the remaining mustard seeds over and press them lightly into the scaloppine.

3. Heat the oil in a heavy skillet large enough to hold the pieces in one layer. Add the veal pieces and cook over very high heat to brown on one side, about 45 seconds. Turn the pieces and cook for about 45 more seconds on the other side.

4. To serve, spoon an equal portion of tomato sauce over the center of 4 warm plates. Arrange 2 pieces of veal neatly over the sauce. Sprinkle with chopped herbs and serve immediately.

FRICASSEE OF FISH WITH WHITE WINE

YIELD: 4 SERVINGS

A fricassee is usually made with chicken, but—as a variation—I make it here with monkfish. I have eliminated the cream that is an ingredient in a classic fricassee.

2 tablespoons olive oil

½ cup chopped celery

16 small button mushrooms

4 tablespoons finely chopped shallots

1 bay leaf

4 sprigs fresh thyme, or 1 teaspoon dried

1 tablespoon finely chopped garlic

2 tablespoons all-purpose flour

2 cups dry white wine, such as as Chardonnay or Chablis

4 cups fish stock or bottled clam juice

2 whole cloves

Salt and freshly ground pepper, to taste

1¾ pounds skinless tilefish or monkfish fillets, or any other white, firm-fleshed fish

4 tablespoons chopped parsley

Garlic Croutons (see page 98)

1. Heat the oil in a large nonstick skillet or saucepan over medium-high heat. Add the celery, mushrooms, shallots, bay leaf, thyme, and garlic. Cook, stirring, until wilted, about 3 minutes.

2. Add the flour and blend well. Stir in the wine, stock, cloves, salt, and pepper. Blend well with a wire whisk. Bring to a boil, reduce the heat, and simmer 10 minutes.

3. Add the fish, bring to a simmer, and cook about 4 minutes or until done. Check for seasoning. Remove the thyme sprigs and bay leaf. Sprinkle with parsley and serve hot with garlic croutons.

MEDALLIONS OF PORK WITH MUSHROOMS

YIELD: 4 SERVINGS

When buying pork, be sure that the meat is light colored, not too red. The whiteness of the meat indicates that the meat is tender and from a young pig. Be sure to trim the meat of any fat.

8 boneless pork loin slices (about 3 ounces each), with all fat removed

Salt and freshly ground pepper, to taste

1 tablespoon olive or vegetable oil

½ cup chopped onion

1 teaspoon chopped garlic

½ pound washed, dried, and thinly sliced mushrooms (if available, wild mushrooms may also be used)

1 tablespoon red wine vinegar

1 cup crushed Italian canned tomatoes

1 sprig fresh rosemary, or ½ teaspoon dried

2 tablespoons chopped fresh basil or parsley

1. Place the pork medallions between 2 pieces of plastic wrap. With a meat pounder or the back of a heavy skillet, pound the medallions lightly so they are all of the same thickness and will cook evenly. Remove the plastic and sprinkle with salt and pepper.

2. Heat the oil in a nonstick skillet large enough to hold the meat in one layer. Turn the meat when well browned, in about 4 minutes, and brown on the other side for 3 minutes more. Pour off the fat and place the onion and garlic around the meat. Cook until wilted, evenly agitating the pan.

3. Add the mushrooms and cook for a few minutes. Add the vinegar, tomatoes, ¼ cup of water, and the rosemary. Check for seasoning, cover, and cook over low heat for 20 minutes.

4. Uncover and reduce the liquid if necessary to produce a thick sauce. Just before serving, sprinkle with basil or parsley.

Fresh Tomato Sauce

YIELD: 2 CUPS

Every August my garden becomes filled with plump, juicy, red tomatoes. This fresh tomato sauce does not require many hours of cooking. Serve it with any kind of meat—it is wonderful with meat loaf and leftover roasts. It freezes well and can be kept for several months.

1½ pounds ripe plum tomatoes
2 tablespoons olive oil
½ cup finely chopped onion
1 tablespoon finely minced garlic
1 sprig fresh rosemary, or 1 teaspoon dried
⅛ teaspoon hot red pepper flakes
Salt and freshly ground pepper, to taste

1. Cut away and discard the cores and seeds of the tomatoes. Cut them into 1-inch cubes; there should be about 3½ cups packed.

2. Heat the oil in a large, heavy saucepan over medium-high heat. Add the onion and garlic, and cook briefly, stirring, until wilted. Do not burn the garlic. Add the tomatoes, bring to a boil, and add the rosemary, red pepper flakes, salt, and pepper. Simmer for about 15 minutes.

3. Remove the rosemary sprig, put the mixture into a food processor, and blend thoroughly. (Or line a saucepan with a large-mesh sieve and pour the sauce into the sieve. Push through, discarding any solids that will not pass through. Or put through a food mill.) Return the sauce to the saucepan, check for seasoning, and serve.

VEAL CASSEROLE WITH VEGETABLES

YIELD: 8 SERVINGS

The veal for this casserole should be lean and cut from the leg or shoulder. This will ensure that the meat has a firm texture and will not fall apart during the cooking process. This casserole is delicious with Baked Rice (see page 165) or noodles, sprinkled with parsley

3½ pounds boneless lean veal, cut into 1½-inch cubes

Salt and freshly ground pepper, to taste

¼ cup all-purpose flour

3 tablespoons olive oil

1½ cups chopped onion

1 teaspoon chopped garlic

½ cup dry white wine

1 cup crushed Italian canned tomatoes

1 cup fresh or canned chicken broth

1 bouquet garni consisting of 4 sprigs parsley, 2 sprigs fresh thyme or ½ teaspoon dried, and 1 bay leaf

1 cup sliced carrots, in 1½-inch lengths

¾ cup sliced celery, in 1½-inch lengths

1 cup sliced turnip, in 1½-inch lengths

¾ pound fresh mushrooms, quartered or left whole if small

2 tablespoons chopped flat-leaf parsley

1. Sprinkle the veal with salt and pepper and dredge in flour. Shake off the excess flour.

2. Heat 2 tablespoons of the olive oil in a large casserole or Dutch oven and add the veal. Cook over medium-high heat, shaking the pot so the meat browns evenly, about 15 minutes. Drain the fat.

3. Add the onion and garlic, and stir. Add the wine, tomatoes, broth, bouquet garni, salt, and pepper. Bring to a boil, scraping the bottom, then cover, reduce the heat, and simmer for about 1 hour.

4. Meanwhile, drop the carrots, celery, and turnip into boiling salted water to cover. Blanch for 1 minute, then drain well.

5. Heat the remaining tablespoon olive oil in a large skillet. Add the mushrooms and blanched vegetables. Cook over high heat, stirring and shaking the skillet, for about 3 minutes. Drain, add to the meat, and stir to blend. Cover and simmer about 15 minutes longer or until the meat is done. Remove the bouquet garni and serve.

FISH STOCK

YIELD: ABOUT 5 CUPS

It is important to use very fresh fish bones to make fish stock. Your local fishmonger can supply you with discarded fish bones and heads. Be sure the gills are removed, along with any bloody parts of the fish. Fish stock can be made ahead of time—it freezes very well for up to two months. I like to freeze it in ice cube trays and use the cubes as needed.

2 pounds very fresh nonoily fish bones, such as striped bass, flounder, fluke, or red snapper, heads included and gills removed

1 cup coarsely chopped celery leaves

1 cup coarsely chopped onion

2 garlic cloves, cut in half

1 bay leaf

2 sprigs thyme, or ½ teaspoon dried

4 sprigs parsley

½ cup chopped green part of leek

1 cup dry white wine

8 peppercorns

1.   Combine all the ingredients in a large pot, add 6 cups of water, bring to a boil over high heat, then reduce the heat and simmer for 20 minutes. Strain and let cool. Refrigerate.

Dutch lobster boats in dock.

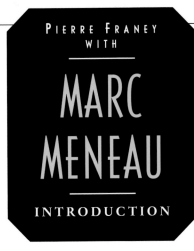

A sense of peacefulness and tranquillity comes over me each time I return to Burgundy, the province of my childhood. Although I left at the age of 14 to become an apprentice cook in Paris, and I have now lived in the United States for more than fifty years, my roots have never died. A part of me will always feel at home when I visit my brother and his family, who farm the land near my hometown of Saint-Vinnemer.

Burgundy is also the home of wonderful vineyards, wines, cheeses, freshwater fish, mushrooms, snails, and restaurants, so it is always a particular pleasure to return. L'Espérance, the elegant restaurant of my good friend Marc Meneau, is frequently one of my stops. It has a three-star rating in the *Guide Michelin*. I have known Marc for many years. He grew up in Saint-Père-sous-Vézelay, a neighboring village of Vézelay that sits atop a rocky crag and is known for its eleventh-century basilica, the starting place for many of the Crusades. The son of a harness maker and grocery store owner, Marc is very proud of his Burgundian heritage, and he helps to promote the region's specialties. The day I visited with him, a local cheese maker came to consult with Marc about a new goat cheese the two men are trying to create with the Vézelay name. After tasting a few samples, Marc's suggested adding a bit of salt and a local herb as a flavoring.

L'Espérance's charming entrance, with its elegant curved steps.

ABOVE: *A most romantic statue inhabits the gardens at Marc Meneau's restaurant, l'Espérance.*
OPPOSITE: *One of l'Espérance's pair of greenhouse dining rooms.* OVERLEAF: *Pierre and Marc Meneau discuss Charollais beef with a local Burgundian breeder.*

Unlike most leading French chefs, Marc did not learn haute cuisine through apprenticeship at top restaurants. He is self-taught, having trained by reading and studying professional cookbooks and developing close ties with several retired chefs and restaurateurs. His success in the kitchen comes from his constant desire to test new ideas, with an eye toward maintaining traditional techniques. For him, the key to a successful cuisine is having great respect for ingredients, proper cooking techniques, and understanding the importance of flavors and the judicious use of seasonings. He sees himself as a country chef creating an innovative menu based on the region's specialties. The restaurant's menu changes each season.

Marc and his wife, Françoise, designed l'Espérance to give their country inn and restaurant a feeling of luxury. Two greenhouse dining rooms and an outdoor terrace overlook a garden filled with trees, flowers, and statues. The restaurant's vegetable and herb garden is off to the side, surrounded by hedges. In the distance is a lovely view of the basilica of Vézelay. Marc has a commanding presence in the kitchen. A tall, gregarious man, he will shout, *"On dit Babar!"* (Say Babar!) from time to time to his young staff and they, in turn, reply *"Babar."* This is all in fun, to make sure they are paying attention to him.

Marc's style of cooking is innovative and original. His menu includes dishes that cater to clients who want a light meal. For example, he serves a warm vegetable tart with an assortment of vegetables cooked in a bouillon and decorated with garlic-flavored spinach leaves as an appetizer. His coquilles St. Jacques (sea scallops) are baked in their shells in a mixture of lemon juice, seawater, a bit of sugar, and olive oil. One of his popular desserts is a puree of raspberries and Champagne, served with sugared rose petals (see page 196). Marc is always inventing new ways of cooking. I include two of his recipes here because they are easy to make and healthful to eat, but even more because they are good examples of how a great three-star chef can reinvent French—indeed, Burgundian—cuisine for today's lighter tastes.

SEA SCALLOPS COOKED IN THEIR OWN SHELLS

YIELD: 4 SERVINGS

In France, sea scallops are sold in their entirety—both shells closed together and the scallop meat still attached inside. It includes the white firm meat and the coral or roe, which is orange in color. In the United States, sea scallops are usually sold out of their shells. But shells to cook in, which are imported from Europe, can be found in any good cooking store and they can be used over and over again.

4 preserved lemons (see recipe following)
1 tablespoon olive oil
1 tablespoon sugar
12 sea scallops in their shells, opened, or large sea scallops from Maine
1½ teaspoons lemon juice
1½ teaspoons fresh or bottled clam juice or seawater
Fresh chervil, for garnish

1. Preheat the oven to 400° F.

2. Slice the lemons lengthwise into quarters, continuing along the "x" already there.

3. Remove the seeds and set aside 12 quarters. Chop the 4 remaining lemon quarters finely. Set aside.

4. In a medium skillet, heat the olive oil and sugar over medium heat. Add the remaining lemon quarters and cook slowly until well caramelized on both sides, 8-10 minutes. Set aside.

5. Sprinkle the chopped lemon evenly over each of the 12 scallops in their shells. Add ⅛ teaspoon lemon juice and ⅛ teaspoon clam juice to each shell. Close each shell and seal by wrapping strips of aluminum foil around the edges (or covering the purchased shells with aluminum foil). The shells should be completely airtight. Place on a baking sheet in the oven for 4-5 minutes. Remove.

6. To serve, remove the foil and open the shells. Remove the top shells. Place 3 scallops on each plate and place a caramelized lemon section on each shell. Garnish with chervil and serve immediately.

PRESERVED LEMONS

YIELD: 4 PRESERVED
LEMONS

¼ cup sea salt
¼ cup sugar
4 lemons
¼ cup lemon juice

1.   Combine the salt and sugar in a small bowl.

2.   Slice an "x" about 1½ inches deep into the top of each lemon. Open slightly with your fingers. Divide the sea salt and sugar mixture equally into 4 mounds and pack the mixture into the openings in the lemons.

3.   Fit the lemons tightly in a sterilized 1-quart mason jar and cover with lemon juice. Seal well so the jar is airtight and leave in the refrigerator for at least 10 days. The lemons can be kept unopened for up to 2 months.

RASPBERRY COULIS WITH CHAMPAGNE AND ROSE PETALS

YIELD: 4 SERVINGS

This recipe is simple to make, but you must prepare the rose petals in advance to allow them to cure in the egg white and sugar mixture. They should be allowed to dry for a minimum of 12 hours.

4 very fragrant untreated pink roses
3 large egg whites, lightly beaten
½ cup granulated sugar
3 pints raspberries
¼ cup Champagne
¼ cup Grand Marnier
Confectioners' sugar, for dusting

1. Separate 24 large, unblemished petals from the roses. Dip in the egg whites, remove any excess, and place on a paper towel on a tray to drain. Then dip the petals in the granulated sugar, taking care to coat both sides well. Place on a piece of parchment paper and allow to dry for at least 12 hours in a dry area at room temperature.

2. Reserve 48 of the best raspberries. Place them separately on a tray.

3. Place the remaining raspberries in a food processor or blender and blend until smooth. Remove and strain through a fine strainer to eliminate most of the seeds. (You can leave a few seeds in the puree so that it has the proper texture of raspberries.) Add the Champagne and blend well.

4. With a pastry brush, gently dab or "paint" each reserved whole raspberry lightly with Grand Marnier. They should be just moistened. Using a fine sieve, dust lightly with confectioners' sugar.

5. To serve, divide the raspberry coulis equally among 4 plates. Place the brushed raspberries over the coulis in a single layer, 12 per plate. Arrange the crystallized rose petals around the edge of each plate and in the center. Serve immediately.

THICK FRESH VEGETABLE SOUP

YIELD: 10-12 SERVINGS

I like soups that are thick, not too watery. To bind this soup and give it substance, I puree a third of it. This eliminates the need to add milk to bind all the ingredients. The remainder is made up of the chopped and diced vegetables. The end result is a soup that has a thick and crunchy texture.

2 tablespoons olive oil
1 cup chopped onion
2 cups coarsely chopped leeks
2 cups coarsely chopped celery
1 tablespoon chopped garlic
2 cups diced carrots
2 cups coarsely chopped white turnips
2 cups peeled and cubed potatoes
2 cups sliced string beans, in 1-inch lengths
2 cups peeled, seeded, and cubed tomatoes
4 cups fresh or canned chicken broth
Salt and freshly ground pepper, to taste
½ cup chopped parsley
½ cup plain low-fat yogurt

1. Heat the olive oil in a large pot and add the onion, leeks, celery, and garlic. Cook over medium heat until wilted. Add the carrots, turnips, potatoes, string beans, tomatoes, chicken broth, 4 cups of water, and salt and pepper. Bring to a simmer, stirring occasionally, and cook for 1 hour.

2. Ladle about one-third of the mixture into a food processor and blend until smooth. Return the blended mixture to the pot. Bring to a boil, then check for seasoning. Sprinkle with chopped parsley and add a dab of yogurt. Serve very hot.

NOTE: This soup is good reheated and freezes well.

FROGS' LEGS WITH GARLIC BUTTER

YIELD: 4 SERVINGS

In Burgundy, one of the classic dishes is frogs' legs. Wild frogs' legs are available in season (fall and early winter), but domestically raised ones are available throughout the year. In the United States, you can order frozen frogs' legs from good fish mongers and in Chinatown. There are many different ways to cook frogs' legs—sautéed, fried, stewed, and even in soufflés! Here, I present a traditional way of serving them.

8 pairs frogs' legs (about 2 pounds)

4 tablespoons olive oil

1 tablespoon finely chopped garlic

2 cups peeled, seeded, and cubed ripe plum tomatoes

Salt and freshly ground pepper, to taste

1 bay leaf

½ cup all-purpose flour

¼ cup low-fat milk

1 tablespoon lemon juice

2 tablespoons finely chopped parsley

1. Cut off and discard the bottom of each leg from the ankle down.

2. Heat 2 tablespoons of the oil in a large, heavy nonstick skillet, add the garlic, and cook, stirring, briefly; do not brown. Add the tomatoes, salt, pepper, and bay leaf. Cook, stirring, for about 5 minutes or until little moisture remains. Set aside and keep warm.

3. Season the flour with salt and pepper. Dip the frogs' legs in the milk, then drain the legs and dredge them, one at a time, in the flour, removing the excess flour.

4. In a heavy nonstick skillet large enough to hold the frogs' legs in one layer, heat the remaining 2 tablespoons oil, then add the frogs' legs. Cook over moderately high heat for 3-4 minutes or until golden brown. Turn and cook on the second side for 3-4 minutes.

5. Divide the frogs' legs evenly among 4 warm serving plates. Sprinkle with the lemon juice. Remove the bay leaf from the tomato and garlic mixture and pour the sauce over the frogs' legs. Sprinkle with chopped parsley.

SPICY SHRIMP AND SQUID SALAD

YIELD: 4 SERVINGS

Squid is considered a great delicacy in France, as well as across Europe. The smaller the squid, the more tender they are and the less cooking they need. If possible, use baby squid and not the large ones, which are normally used for deep-frying.

¾ pound raw medium shrimp

1 pound baby or medium squid

4 tablespoons red wine vinegar

1 bay leaf

½ teaspoon hot red pepper flakes

Salt, to taste

8 whole black peppercorns

¼ cup olive oil

1 tablespoon chopped fresh oregano, or ½ teaspoon dried

1 tablespoon finely chopped garlic

2 tablespoons lemon juice

½ cup chopped celery

1 large red bell pepper, cored, seeded, and cut into ½-inch-long thin strips

¼ cup drained capers

¼ cup chopped flat-leaf parsley

1. Peel and devein the shrimp.

2. Cut off the tentacles and eyes of the squid. Pull and squeeze out the beak. Remove the skin by holding the squid under cold water and rubbing with coarse salt, or simply by pulling and rubbing with the fingers. Rinse the shell of the squid, drain thoroughly, and cut the squid crosswise into 1-inch rings.

3. Place the shrimp and squid in a large saucepan, add 2 tablespoons vinegar, ½ cup water, the bay leaf, red pepper flakes, salt, and peppercorns. Bring to a boil and cook about 2 minutes, taking care not to overcook. Set aside for at least 30 minutes to cool.

4. Remove the shrimp and squid rings and place in a salad bowl. Add the remaining 2 tablespoons vinegar and the olive oil, oregano, garlic, lemon juice, celery, bell pepper, capers, and parsley. Toss well to blend, and serve.

VEAL CHOPS WITH WILD MUSHROOMS

YIELD: 4 SERVINGS

When buying veal, make sure that the meat and the fat are white in color. The light color indicates that the veal was milk-fed, which ensures the tenderness and good quality of the meat. Noodles or rice go well with this dish.

4 veal chops (about ¾ pound each), with most of the fat removed
Salt and freshly ground pepper, to taste
¼ cup all-purpose flour
1 tablespoon olive oil
¾ pound shiitake or other wild mushrooms, cleaned
2 tablespoons finely chopped shallots
½ cup Madeira wine
1 tablespoon butter

1. Sprinkle the chops with salt and pepper, then dredge them on both sides in the flour and shake off the excess.

2. Heat the oil in a large, heavy nonstick skillet. Add the chops and cook about 5 minutes over medium-high heat or until the chops are nicely browned on one side. Turn and cook on the second side 8-10 minutes more. Do not overcook. Transfer the chops to a warm platter.

3. Remove most of the fat from the pan. Add the mushrooms, salt, and pepper and cook, stirring and tossing them, until they become wilted, 4-5 minutes. If there is any fat left, pour it from the pan.

4. Add the shallots and cook, stirring, until wilted. Add the Madeira and reduce liquid by one-half. Add any juices that may have accumulated around the chops. Swirl in the butter, add the chops, and cook for about 3 minutes to heat through. Serve the chops with the sauce spooned over.

PEPPERY HAMBURGERS WITH RED WINE SAUCE

YIELD: 4 SERVINGS

The American in me loves to eat hamburgers. The best meat for them is square chuck, which comes from the front leg of the steer and is quite lean. I never buy meat that is already ground; I prefer to have the butcher grind it. If that's not possible, then I grind the meat myself at home in a meat grinder. This ensures freshness and less fat because I remove excess fat myself.

1½ pounds lean, freshly ground beef chuck

2 teaspoons olive oil

¾ cup finely chopped onion

1 teaspoon finely chopped garlic

1 tablespoon chili powder

1 teaspoon ground cumin

1 teaspoon freshly ground pepper or coarsely cracked black peppercorns

⅛ teaspoon hot red pepper flakes

½ teaspoon Worcestershire sauce

Salt, to taste

1 tablespoon butter

2 tablespoons chopped shallots

½ cup dry red wine

¼ cup fresh or canned chicken broth

2 tablespoons chopped parsley

1. Place the meat in a mixing bowl.

2. Heat the oil in a small cast-iron skillet, add the onion and cook, stirring, until wilted. Add the garlic and cook briefly, stirring. Do not let the garlic burn. Remove from the heat and let cool.

3. Add the cooled onion mixture, chili powder, cumin, ground pepper, red pepper flakes, Worcestershire sauce, and salt to the meat and blend well. Divide the mixture into 4 patties of equal size.

4. Heat a heavy cast-iron skillet large enough to hold all the patties in one layer. Do not add fat of any kind. When the skillet is quite hot and smoking, add the patties. Cook until well browned on one side, then turn and cook 3 minutes more on the second side for medium rare. Cook longer if desired. Transfer to a warm platter.

5. Heat the butter in a small skillet. Add the shallots and cook, stirring, for 1 minute. Add the wine and broth and let cook until reduced about ¼ cup. Check for seasoning and sprinkle with parsley. Serve immediately.

NOTE: If a heavy black cast-iron pan is not available, use a heavy-bottomed fry pan.

BEEF BURGUNDY

YIELD: 8-10 SERVINGS

This is one of my favorite winter dishes. It can be made without marinating the meat, but the result will be less flavorful. Be sure to use a heavy pot with a tight-fitting lid, so the liquid does not reduce too much and the bottom does not brown.

5 pounds lean beef stew meat, such as round, chuck, or brisket, with excess fat removed and meat cut into 1½-inch cubes

Salt and freshly ground pepper, to taste

½ pound onions, coarsely cut (about 2 cups)

1 large carrot, coarsely cut

1 tablespoon finely chopped garlic

2 whole cloves

1 bouquet garni made with 4 sprigs fresh thyme, 1 bay leaf, 1 small sprig rosemary, and 6 sprigs parsley, all tied together

4 cups red Burgundy wine

2 tablespoons olive or vegetable oil

4 tablespoons all-purpose flour

1 cup fresh or canned beef broth

18 small white onions

1 pound whole small mushrooms

1. Place the meat in a large bowl with the salt and pepper. Add the onions, carrot, garlic, cloves, bouquet garni, and wine. Blend well and cover with plastic wrap. Let marinate in the refrigerator for about 6 hours.

2. Remove the meat from marinade and drain in a colander. Drain the vegetables and reserve the marinade. Place the vegetables and bouquet garni in a cheesecloth and tie with a string.

3. In a large Dutch oven or heavy casserole, heat the oil over high heat. Add the meat and stir quickly, until the meat loses its red color. Drain the fat. Sprinkle the flour over and blend well with a spatula until all the meat is coated, about 5 minutes. Add the marinade and broth, bring to a boil, and blend well. Add the vegetables in the cheesecloth and simmer for 1 hour, stirring and scraping the bottom. Skim the surface of any fat.

4. Add the small onions and mushrooms; check seasoning. Simmer for about 30 minutes or until the meat is tender, stirring and scraping the bottom often. Check for seasoning. The meat should be well done; if not, cook longer.

5. Remove the bouquet garni and serve the meat on warm plates with noodles, rice, parsley, or potatoes.

NOTE: If the stew persists in bubbling vigorously even on low heat, use a flame tamer to diffuse the heat.

ENDIVE MEUNIÈRE

YIELD: 4 SERVINGS

This dish can be made ahead of time. After braising the endive, cover and refrigerate until ready to use. Then, sauté them quickly in a little butter and the liquid from cooking the endive.

4 large heads Belgian endive
2 tablespoons butter
Juice of 1 lemon
½ teaspoon sugar
Salt and freshly ground pepper, to taste
1 tablespoon finely chopped parsley

1. Trim off and discard any discolored leaves from the endive. Wash with cold water and drain.

2. Melt 1 tablespoon of the butter in a medium nonstick skillet with a tight-fitting lid. Add the endive—they should be in one layer. Add the lemon juice, ⅓ cup water, sugar, salt, and pepper. Cover and bring to a boil. Simmer for 15-20 minutes or until tender. Drain well.

3. Melt the remaining tablespoon butter in a nonstick skillet large enough to hold the endive in one layer. Add the endive, brown on one side, then brown on the other side. Sprinkle with the parsley. Serve hot.

NOODLES WITH MUSHROOMS

YIELD: 4 SERVINGS

These tasty noodles can be served with a stew, such as Beef Burgundy (see previous page), or as a separate pasta course.

1 tablespoon butter
1 tablespoon finely chopped shallot
¼ pound sliced tiny mushrooms
Salt and freshly ground pepper, to taste
½ pound thin noodles
4 tablespoons grated Parmesan, Gruyère, or Comté cheese

1. Heat the butter in a medium saucepan. Add the shallot and cook briefly, stirring. Add the mushrooms, salt, and pepper. Cook over medium-high heat, stirring until the mushrooms give up most of their liquid and are slightly browned, 5-6 minutes. Set aside.

2. Meanwhile, cook the noodles in boiling salted water in a large pot according to the package instructions. Do not overcook. Drain, then place in a bowl and add the mushrooms, their liquid, and the Parmesan cheese. Blend well and serve.

VEGETABLE TART

—

YIELD: 4 SERVINGS

This recipe was inspired by a recipe of Marc Meneau. Little cooking liquid is used; therefore, it is important that the carrots, beans, and turnips be fresh and young—and not dried out.

1 12-ounce sheet of store-bought fresh or frozen puff pastry
4 small carrots (about ½ pound)
4 small white turnips (about ½ pound), with 2 inches of greens
¼ pound fresh small green beans
1 tablespoon butter
1 tablespoon olive oil
8 small scallions, trimmed
1 teaspoon chopped garlic
¼ pound fresh wild mushrooms, such as morels, chanterelles, or shiitake
¼ teaspoon ground cumin
8 sprigs of fresh chervil
Salt and freshly ground pepper, to taste

1. Preheat the oven to 375° F.

2. Place the puff pastry in a 10-inch tart or quiche pan, making sure to line the sides as well. Trim off excess. Place a sheet of aluminum foil over the bottom and cover with a layer of dried beans, about ¾ cup. Bake in the oven for 15 minutes, or until the sides become lightly brown. Remove the beans and the aluminum foil and bake for another 5 minutes, until the bottom is brown. Remove from the oven and set aside.

3. Trim and peel the carrots, then cut them into quarters lengthwise.

4. Peel the turnips, leaving about 2 inches of greens attache. Trim the green beans.

5. Heat the butter and oil in a large skillet with a tight-fitting lid. Add the scallions and garlic and cook briefly, stirring. Add the mushrooms and sauté for about 5 minutes. Add the carrots, turnips, and beans. Add about ¼ cup water, the cumin, half the chervil, and salt and pepper. Cover tightly, bring to a boil, reduce the heat, and simmer for 20 minutes. Place in the tart shell, and return to the oven for 5 minutes or until warm. Garnish with the remaining chervil and serve immediately.

DATE-NUT COOKIES

YIELD: ABOUT 60 COOKIES

These cookies are a speciality of my wife, Betty.

2 large egg whites
1 cup sugar
1 cup chopped walnuts or hazelnuts
1 cup chopped pitted dates

1. Preheat the oven to 275° F.

2. Beat the egg whites until stiff. Add the sugar gradually and beat well.

3. Add the nuts and dates, folding in gently. Drop by half-teaspoonfuls onto well-greased cookie sheets. Bake 8-10 minutes or until lightly browned. Watch carefully so they don't become too brown.

PEACHES BAKED IN GRENADINE SYRUP

YIELD: 8-10 SERVINGS

I bake the peaches with their pits because the pits give a nice flavor and help the peaches retain their shape.

8 ripe unblemished peaches
1¼ cups sugar
2 teaspoons vanilla extract, or 1 vanilla bean split in half lengthwise
1 stick cinnamon
3 tablespoons grenadine syrup
5 tablespoons Grand Marnier

1. Preheat the oven to 425° F.

2. Drop the peaches into a large quantity of boiling water. Let them simmer for 45 seconds-2 minutes, depending on ripeness, then drain immediately and pull off the skins with a paring knife. If properly blanched, the skins of the peaches should come off easily.

3. Place the peaches in a flameproof baking dish just large enough to hold them in one layer.

4. Combine 1¼ cups water, the sugar, vanilla, and cinnamon in a medium saucepan and bring to a boil. Simmer for 5 minutes, then pour over the peaches and add the grenadine syrup and 2 tablespoons Grand Marnier. Bring to a boil on top of the stove, then place in the oven to bake for 30 minutes, basting the peaches frequently with the syrup. Remove the peaches to a serving dish.

5. Cook the sauce on the stovetop for 10 minutes over high heat to reduce it. Add the remaining Grand Marnier, then pour the sauce over the peaches. Refrigerate peaches until thoroughly chilled and serve with syrup around them.

ACKNOWLEDGMENTS

There are many people, friends and family, who helped with this book and the accompanying television series. First, I would like to thank Michel Roux and the Grand Marnier Foundation and Patricia Barroll of Carillon Importers, Ltd., for their enthusiasm and their financial support. Executive Producer and Director Charles Pinsky of Frappé Productions, Inc., brought his usual expertise to bear in making this project such a success. And I am grateful to Maryland Public Television—in particular to John T. Potthast, Executive in Charge of Production, and Margaret Sullivan, Coordinating Producer. My agent, Roger Vergnes of Copperplate Press, was an enormous help to me. Of course, I am particularly indebted to my old and new friends, the chefs and restaurateurs whose recipes and restaurants provide the framework for this project.

My television crew was indispensable, putting in long hours as we traveled around Europe. A big thank you to Anna Klinger, Bruno Chataigner, Terry Williams, Pekka Littow, Don Barto, and Bill and Anu Echikson. In addition, I am grateful to Regis Bulow of the Relais et Chateaux hotel and restaurant chain and to the representatives of the various tourist offices who served as guides when we visited each country.

Special thanks to photographers Martin Brigdale and Jean Cazals, who accompanied us throughout Europe. At Artisan, it was a pleasure to work with the publisher, Leslie Stoker, and my editor, Ann ffolliott. Special thanks to the Artisan team—Hope Koturo, Beth Wareham, Felice Primeau, Christina Sheldon, and Dana Lostritto—and to others who made invaluable contributions to the book—Carole Berglie, Marcia Pomerantz, Katherine Pulver, and Catherine Dorsey. Joel Avirom, Meghan Day Healey, and Jason Snyder provided the beautiful design.

Last but not least, a big thank you to my family for their love and wholehearted support of this latest project. My wife, Betty, was at my side throughout the voyage through Europe, always there to take notes, give advice, and be my right hand.

Featured Restaurants

Paul Bocuse
5, Pied de la Plage
69660 Collonges-au-Mont-d'Or
France
Tel. (33) 72-42-90-90
Fax (33) 72-27-85-87

Michel Guérard
Les prés d'Eugénie
40320 Eugénie-les-Bains
France
Tel. (33) 58-05-06-07
Fax (33) 58-51-10-10

Restaurante Arzak
Alto de Miracruz, 21
San Sebastián
Tel. (43) 27-84-65
Fax (43) 27-27-53

Hotel Arts
Carrer de la Marina, 19-21
08005 Barcelona
Spain
Tel. 800-241-3333
Newport Room:
Tel. (93) 221 10 00
Fax (93) 221 10 70

El Bulli
Cala Montjoy, Roses
Spain
Tel. (72) 15-04-17
Fax (72) 15-07-17

Dal Pescatore
46013 Canneto sull'Oglio
Italy
Tel. (39) 376-72-30-01
Fax (39) 376-70-30-4

Ristorante la Greppia
Via Garibaldi, 39
43100 Parma
Italy
Tel. (39) 0521-233686

Girardet
1 route d'Yverdon
Crissier
Switzerland
Tel. (21) 634-05-05
Fax (21) 634-05-06

Schwarzwald-Stube
Hotel Traube Tonbach
Tonbach Str.237
Baiersbronn, D 72270
Germany
Tel. (49) 7442-4920
Fax (49) 7442-492692

Restaurant Bareiss
Hotel Bareiss
Gretenbehlveg 14
Baiersbronn, D 72270
Germany
Tel. (49) 7442-47-0
Fax (49) 7442-47-320

Scholteshof
Kermstraat 130
3512 Stevoort
Belgium
Tel. (32) 11-25-02-02
Fax (32) 11-25-43-28

Comme Chez Soi
Place Rouppe, 23
B-1000 Brussels
Belgium
Tel. (32) 2-512-29-21
Fax (32) 2-511-80-52

Manoir Inter Scaldes
Zandweg 2
4416 NA Kruiningen
Netherlands
Tel. (31) (113) 381-753
Fax (31) (113) 381-763

L'Espérance
89450 Saint-Père-sous-Vézelay
France
Tel. (33) 86-33-20-45
Fax (33) 86-33-26-15

CONVERSION CHARTS

VOLUME EQUIVALENTS

These are not exact equivalents for the American cups and spoons, but have been rounded up or down slightly to make measuring easier.

American	Metric	Imperial
¼ t	1.25 ml	
½ t	2.5 ml	
1 t	5 ml	
½ T (1½ t)	7.5 ml	
1 T (3 t)	15 ml	
¼ cup (4 T)	60 ml	2 fl. oz
⅓ cup (5 T)	75 ml	2½ fl oz
½ cup (8 T)	125 ml	4 fl oz
⅔ cup (10 T)	150 ml	5 fl oz (¼ pint)
¾ cup (12 T)	175 ml	6 fl oz
1 cup (16 T)	250 ml	8 fl oz
1¼ cups	300 ml	10 fl oz
1½ cups	350 ml	12 fl oz
1 pint (2 cups)	500 ml	16 fl oz
1 quart (4 cups)	1 litre	1¾ pints

WEIGHT EQUIVALENTS

The metric weights given in this chart are not exact equivalents, but have been rounded up or down slightly to make measuring easier.

Avoirdupois	Metric	Avoirdupois	Metric
¼ oz	7 g	12 oz	350 g
½ oz	15 g	13 oz	375 g
1 oz	30 g	14 oz	400 g
2 oz	60 g	15 oz	425 g
3 oz	90 g	16 oz (1 lb)	450 g
4 oz	115 g	1 lb 2 oz	500 g
5 oz	150 g	1½ lb	750 g
6 oz	175 g	2 lb	900 g
7 oz	200 g	2¼ lb	1 kg
8 oz (½ lb)	225 g	3 lb	1.4 kg
9 oz	250 g	4 lb	1.8 kg
10 oz	300 g	4½ lb	2 kg
11 oz	325 g		

OVEN TEMPERATURE EQUIVALENTS

Oven	° F.	° C.	Gas Mark
very cool	250-275	130-140	½–1
cool	300	150	2
warm	325	170	3
moderate	350	180	4
moderately hot	375	190	5
	400	200	6
hot	425	220	7
very hot	450	230	8
	475	250	9

EGGS

Unless otherwise noted, all recipes in this book use American large size eggs, which are equivalent to British standard-size eggs.

FLOUR

American all-purpose flour is milled from a mixture of hard and soft wheats, whereas British plain flour is made mainly from soft wheat. To achieve a near equivalent to American all-purpose flour, use half British plain flour and half strong bread flour.

SUGAR

In the recipes in this book, if sugar is called for it is assumed to be granulated, unless otherwise specified. American granulated sugar is finer than British granulated, closer to caster sugar.

INGREDIENTS AND EQUIPMENT GLOSSARY

British English and American English are not always the same, particularly in the kitchen. The following ingredients and equipment used in this book are pretty much the same on both sides of the Atlantic, but have different names:

American	British
bell pepper	sweet pepper (capsicum)
broiler/to broil	grill/to grill
celery stalk	celery stick
confectioners' sugar	icing sugar
cornstarch	cornflour
scallion	spring onion
skillet	frying pan

INDEX

DESIGNED BY JOEL AVIROM

DESIGN ASSISTANTS: JASON SNYDER AND MEGHAN DAY HEALEY

TYPEFACES IN THIS BOOK ARE DANTE AND CASABLANCA

PRINTED AND BOUND BY

ARNOLDO MONTADORI EDITORE S.P.A.

VERONA, ITALY